Adeline Myers

GLOBAL MEATBALLS

AROUND THE WORLD IN 100+ BOUNDARY BREAKING RECIPES

FROM BEEF TO BEAN AND ALL DELICIOUS THINGS IN BETWEEN

Quarry Books
100 Cummings Center, Suite 406L
Beverly, MA 01915

quarrybooks.com • quarryspoon.com

© 2015 by Quarry Books

First published in the United States of America in 2015 by
Quarry Books, a member of
Quarto Publishing Group USA Inc.
100 Cummings Center
Suite 406-L
Beverly, Massachusetts 01915-6101
Telephone: (978) 282-9590
Fax: (978) 283-2742
www.quarrybooks.com
Visit www.QuarrySPOON.com and help us celebrate food
and culture one spoonful at a time!

10 9 8 7 6 5 4 3 2 1

ISBN: 978-1-59253-954-3

Digital edition published in 2015
eISBN: 978-1-62788-227-9

Library of Congress Cataloging-in-Publication Data

Myers, Adeline, author.
Global meatballs: around the world in 100+ boundary
breaking recipes, from beef to bean and all delicious things in
between / Adeline Myers. Pages cm

ISBN 978-1-59253-954-3 (paperback) –
ISBN 978-1-62788-227-9 (digital edition)
1. Meatballs. 2. Cooking (Meat) I. Title.
TX749.M956 2015
641.6'6–dc23
2014025569

Design: www.studioink.co.uk
Cover Image: www.studioink.co.uk
Food Styling: Natasha St. Hailare Taylor
Photography: Glenn Scott
Courtesy of Shutterstock.com: pages 14, 60, 71, 76, 78, 86,
    87, 98, 121, 129, 139, 142, 146, 153, 166

Printed in China

For Michael

Contents

Introduction 8

1 Meatballs

Snacks/Appetizers

Chorizo and White Wine Tapas Meatballs (Spain) 16

Bulgur and Lamb Meatball Snacks (Brazil) 18

North Indian Potato and Lamb Kofta (India) 19

Sesame Lamb Meatballs with Cucumber Mint Yogurt Dip (Middle East) 21

Picnic Favorite Spiced Frikkadels (South Africa) 22

Lion's Head Meatballs (China) 23

Soups/Stews

Italian Wedding Soup (USA) 24

Deconstructed Red Kubbeh Soup with Couscous (Jewish) 27

Easy Yellow Curry with Thai Meatballs (Thailand) 28

Lemongrass Pork Meatball Soup (Cambodia) 30

Sopa de Albondigas (Costa Rica) 31

Spiced Meatball, Yam, and Peanut Stew over Couscous (West Africa) 33

Louisiana Alligator Meatball Gumbo (USA) 34

Meatball Chowder (Mongolia) 35

Cassoulet with Duck Confit and Pork Meatballs (France) 36

Cajun Meatball Stew (USA) 38

Sandwiches

Bacon and Onion Meatball Sliders (USA) 39

Pork Meatballs in Lettuce Cups with Chili Dipping Sauce (Laos) 41

Báhn Mi Meatball Sandwich on Baguette (Vietnam) 42

Pita Sandwiches with Lamb Kefta, Harissa and Chopped Salad (Morocco) 44

Open-Faced Meatball Sandwich, Frikadeller Smørrebrød (Denmark) 45

Melting Messy Meatball Sub (USA) 47

Mains

Meatballs with Tomato Sauce (Southern Italy) 48

Little Italy Spaghetti and Meatballs (USA) 51

Albondigas with Tomato Sauce (Venezuela) 52

Lamb Meatballs with Baked Yogurt Sauce (Greece) 53

Grilled Beef Meatballs with Chimichurri Sauce (Argentina) 55

Meatball Kebabs (Turkey) 56

Grilled BBQ Meatballs (Australia) 57

Pistachio Lamb Meatballs with Sweet and Sour Pomegranate Glaze (Middle East) 58

Jewel-Stuffed Bison Meatballs with Mustard Glaze (Ancient Rome) 60

Smoky, Spiced, Sumac Meatballs, Ketzitzot (Israel) 61

Green Kofta Curry (India) 62

Grilled Apricot and Ostrich Kebabs (South Africa) 63

Apple and Fennel Kotlecky (Russia) 64

Spicy Sichuan Meatballs (China) 65

Poached Meatballs in Caper Cream Sauce, Konigsberg Klopse (Germany) 66

Swedish Meatballs (Sweden) 69

Buckwheat Meatballs with Mushroom Gravy (Poland) 70

Venison Meatballs with Wild Berries (USA) 71

Provençal Rabbit and Sage Meatballs with Roasted Garlic Aioli and Potatoes (France) 72

Arctic Circle Elk Meatballs (Scandinavia) 74

Lamb and Apricot Meatballs with Greek Yogurt (England) 75

Rich Meatballs and Gravy (France) 76

Nose to Tail Offal Meatballs (England) 77

2 Poultry Balls

Soup/Stews

Mama's Chicken Meatball Soup (Ukraine) 80

Red Pozole with Chicken Meatballs (Mexico) 81

Xim Xim Nutty Chicken Meatball and Shrimp Stew (Brazil) 82

Yellow Gundi Chicken Meatball Soup (Persia) 83

Red Curry with Eggplant, Greens, and Meatballs (Thailand) 85

Mains

Japanese Yakitori Chicken Meatballs (Japan) 86

Chicken Meatballs with Olives, Feta, and Sun-Dried Tomatoes (Mediterranean) 87

Taco Chicken Meatballs with Red Salsa Rice (Mexico) 88

Chermoula Chicken Boulettes (Morocco) 90

Duck, Prosciutto, and Prune Stuffed Meatballs (USA) 91

Thanksgiving Stuffing Turkey Meatballs with Cranberry Sauce (USA) 93

Orange Duck Meatballs with Celery Root Purée (Australia) 94

Duck Curry Meatballs with Spicy Onion Chutney (India) 97

3 Fish Balls

Appetizers/Snacks

Crunchy Wild Shrimp Balls (China) 100

Salted Codfish Fritters, Buñelos de Bacala (Spain) 102

Fish Hash Balls (Cuba) 103

Fried Fish Balls with Grilled Pineapple Salsa (USA) 105

Beer-Battered Fish Balls with Chili Dipping Sauce (Australia) 106

Steamed Spicy Mussel Balls of Mumbai (India) 108

Soups/Stews

Kerala Red Curry with Fish Balls (Southern India) 109

Spicy Fish Balls in Tomato Vegetable Stew (West Africa) 110

Fish and Yucca Dumplings with Callaloo (Caribbean) 111

Moroccan Chard and Chickpeas Fish Ball Tagine (Morocco) 113

Monkfish Balls in a Tagine of Tomato, Olives, and Preserved Lemon (Tunisia) 114

San Francisco Crab Ball Chowder (USA) 117

Fish Ball and Noodle Soup (Korea) 118

Mains

Catfish Hush Puppies with Coleslaw (USA) 120

Baked Fish Balls with Frankfurt Green Sauce (Germany) 121

Fiskeboller (Scandinavia) 123

Herbed Swordfish Balls, Psarokeftethes (Greece) 124

New England Codfish Balls with Tartar Sauce (USA) 125

Codfish Fritters with Green Brazilian Rice (Brazil) 126

Fish Albondigas in Poblano Salsa (Mexico) 128

Tonga Yam and Fish Fritters with Mango Salsa (South Pacific) 129

Quick Potato, Corn, and Tuna Fish Balls (Australia) 131

Ginger and Scallion Namero Mackerel Balls (Japan) 132

Poached Salmon Balls (Scandinavia) 135

Sicilian Tuna Balls with Roasted Tomatoes (Italy) 136

Lobster and Grits Croquettes with Garlic Leafy Greens (USA) 137

4 Veggie Balls

Appetizers/Snacks

Puffy Fried Tofu Balls, Agedashi Tofu (Japan) 140

Green Plantain and Cheese Balls, Bolón de Verde (Ecuador) 142

Ginger and Chile Lentil Fritters (India) 143

Walnut, Za'atar, and Eggplant Kufteh (Morocco) 144

Tapas Chickpea Balls (Spain) 145

Red Lentil and Bulgur Kufteh in Lettuce Leaves (Middle East) 146

Onigiri Rice Balls with Smoked Salmon and Sesame Seeds (Japan) 147

Next Day Baked Aranchini (Italy) 148

Soups

Potato Ball and Milk Soup (Russia) 149

Vegetarian Matzo Ball Soup (Jewish) 150

Mains

Falafel with Mint Yogurt Sauce (Middle East) 151

Quinoa Zucchini and Sweet Potato Balls (USA) 152

Ruby Beet Balls (Georgia) 153

Tuscan Cannellini Bean Balls (USA) 155

Abundant Vegetable Tofu Balls in Kombu Broth, "Ganmodoki" (Japan) 156

Lentil Balls with Spices, Lemon Pesto, and Tahini Sauce (Middle East) 159

Scallion Tofu Balls with Ginger Glaze (Japan) 160

Potato Balls Stuffed with Cheese (Ukraine) 163

Zucchini Balls with Tomato Curry Sauce (India) 164

Mushroom Garlic Tofu Balls in Tomato Sauce (USA) 166

Resources 168

Index 170

Acknowledgments 174

About the Author 175

Introduction

The basic ingredients of meatballs are simple: protein, eggs, breadcrumbs, and seasoning.

We all love meatballs. They evoke memories of our grandmothers' kitchens, of family dinners, and of holidays. Meatballs have a charming quality. The humble, misshapen rounds are quaint, delightful, and mysterious. Meatballs feel definitively handmade, a mark of time and love.

The meatball is more than a round ball of meat. On our wide planet they are made with meats, fish, grains, vegetables, and legumes. Their names shine with possibility: albondigas, bitki, frikkadel, kefta, kofta, kufteh, kotlecky, klopsiki, pulpety, polpetes . . . .

The meatball has range and is not as homely as we may think. In cultures where meat has historically been abundant, like Northern Europe, Scandinavia, and North America, meatballs are common comfort food, made with few ingredients and very little fuss by all households. Where meat was scarce, such as in Italy, meatballs included lots of bread, were made on festival days, and were usually small and very special. Where meatballs were made for the banquet tables of kings and noblemen, they were filled with riches like pine nuts, pomegranates, and innumerable spices.

The beauty of a meatball is in its simplicity.

Ground/mashed protein: meat, fish, vegetables, or legumes
Light texture: bread, bread crumbs, flour, starch, or grains
Moisture: milk, water, yogurt, or wine
Binder: whole egg, yolk, white flour, or starch
Depth of flavor: herbs, spices, or salt

These are only guidelines. Many meatballs are made with only the ground protein and spices, with no egg, wheat, or milk. If you are cooking for someone whose dietary choices limit things like egg, gluten, dairy, or meat, you will find plenty of options among the recipes of this book. And do as our meatball-loving ancestors did and change, modify, and make the meatball local to where you live.

I have arranged this book by protein: meat, poultry, fish, and vegetable. Arranged within each chapter are courses: appetizers, soups/stews, sandwiches, and mains. Lastly, within each course, recipes are arranged from light to rich in flavor. Meatballs with sauces of fresh herbs precede creamy gravy dishes. Happy meatball making!

SMALL   **MEDIUM**   **LARGE**

Size and Cooking Time

Each recipe indicates the recommended size of the meatball. Cooking times given are for the indicated size. If you make smaller or larger balls, be sure to shorten or lengthen your cooking time.

Three Tips for Forming the Balls
- Make them compact, without large cracks.
- Use wet hands for neat results; they will be far less sticky.
- Make them the same size, so they finish cooking at the same time.

And How to Stuff Them
Stuffed meatballs are a real surprise, often filled with melting cheese. They are easy to make.

a. Form the mixture into a ball.

b. Using a thumb, press a deep hole into the ball. Place the filling inside.

c. Take a little more of the mixture and use it to cover the filling. Roll the whole thing so it is round and compact.

How Do I Know when the Balls are Done?
Meatballs are typically cooked well done. Eventually, you will be able to tell they are done just by poking a meatball. Until then, you can use two approaches.

1) Cut one meatball in half. If it is the same opaque color all the way through, it is done. If not, cook for more time.

2) Use a meat thermometer; recommended USDA temperatures are higher for ground meats than for whole cuts of meat. This is because potential contamination is not only on the surface but on the insides of ground meat. Buy good meat from well-maintained farms and you will worry about this less.

How Do I Freeze Balls?

It's simple, and once they are in your freezer, they are an easy meal, ready to go in just moments. Remember to label them so you remember what they are! I will lay out the variations here:

Basic Freezing Method:

Lay the balls on a baking tray, not touching one another. Freeze, uncovered, for 2 or more hours. It is okay to leave them like this overnight. Remove them from the baking tray into a plastic freezer bag, press the air out, and seal. This way they don't freeze in one big lump. They're best eaten from the freezer within 4 months for freshness.

COOKED MEAT OR VEGGIE BALLS:

Use the Basic Freezing Method. Thaw in the fridge, reheat in an oven, or simmer in a sauce until warmed through.

RAW MEAT, FISH, OR VEGGIE BALLS:

Use the Basic Freezing Method. When ready to eat, thaw in the fridge or put frozen balls right into a hot oven, sauce, soup, or deep-fry. You will have to cook them just a bit longer than usual because they are coming from frozen.

BALLS WITH SAUCE:

If they are in sauce, presumably they are already cooked. When cooled, scoop into freezer bags with the sauce and seal so all the air is pressed out. To reheat, thaw and simmer until warmed through.

PAR-COOKED MEATBALLS:

This technique saves the last stage of cooking until after the freezer to eliminate the worry the meatballs may dry out or overcook when reheated. Label the bag so you remember they are only half-cooked. This applies well to meatballs cooked in a skillet before being put in a sauce or baked. Sauté, fry, or bake the meatballs as directed. Allow them to cool and use the Basic Freezing Method. When ready to eat, simmer them in sauce or put them directly into the oven. Cook until entirely cooked through.

FREEZING FISH BALLS:

Fish balls can get watery or tough after freezing. This is the best bet: Cook the fish balls by boiling or frying, as the recipe specifies. Remove, drain, and cool on a tray. Follow the Basic Freezing Method. When ready to eat, remove from the freezer and simmer directly in sauce. If serving simply poached, as in fiskeboller, thaw first. Then simmer in water until warmed through.

I Want to Grind My Meat at Home!

More power to you! It can mean more cleanup, but if you have the time and equipment, then you have all the power in your hands. The recipes in this book are designed with preground meat in mind. Buy good cuts of meat from your butcher. Carefully remove any silver skin, which can have a gamey flavor, especially in older wild animals. Cut the meat into chunks that will fit into the grinder chute. Cold meat grinds more easily than warm: the fattier the meat, the truer this is. Chill the cubes of meat very well or freeze them for 30 minutes to an hour, not so they are frozen solid, but so they are very cold. Put it all through your meat grinder. Sometimes it is nice to send it through a second time for a very fine result.

* If the recipes call for a blend of different meats, grind them together, as they will be better incorporated.

* Some recipes call for grated onion or vegetables. Put these through the grinder with the meat! This was typical in older recipes when ground meat was not commonly available at the market and people ground meats at home.

Deep-Frying at Home?

Deep-frying is intimidating for many of us; however, in many parts of the world, deep-frying is the go-to method of cooking. While it is not as healthy as steaming, if done well and as a special treat, it need not be worrisome. Some people, like me, worry about the amount of oil or the cleanup. I have found an easy way to cut down on both. Use a wok! I think a wok is genius, and I don't do it any other way. My wok is made of thick metal and is very sturdy on my stove. The concave, round shape allows me to deep-fry with less than a cup of oil! It has high sides and a wide outside lip so the oil splatter stays fairly contained. The one drawback is the small pool of oil makes it necessary to cook everything in smaller batches. But it goes so quickly, I don't mind.

Food cooks so quickly when deep-fried because oil is a first-rate conductor of heat. (This is also why it burns so badly when you touch it.) The key to good deep-frying is to have your oil hot enough. Hot oil at 350°F (180°C) or 375°F (190°C) will instantly heat the water molecules inside your meatball to the boiling point, causing it to steam from within. All this steam is expelled in violent bubbles, like an explosion, which doesn't allow the oil to move inside. Cool oil results in oily food because the oil penetrates before the water is turned to steam.

Allow the oil to cool in the pan and pour it into a jar to save for next time. I find that deep-frying fish balls imparts a fishy smell to the oil, and the oil should be used only for other fish recipes or discarded. Discard your oil after two or three uses or if it turns very dark or smells "off."

Three Tips to Follow:

* Lower the food into the oil with a slotted spoon or roll it down the side of a wok so it doesn't splash.

* Don't crowd the oil. Each piece of food added to the oil drops the temperature by several degrees.

* When the bubbles subside and are less violent, this indicates the food is cooked. Remove and drain.

1

Meatballs

Beef, pork, veal, lamb, goat, ostrich . . . from the usual to the exotic, we love meat. It's delicious, satisfying, and a canvas for the flavors of the world, enriched by spices and sauces from pole to pole. In every neighborhood, meatballs are rolled up and cooked on grills, open fires, or skillets; deep-fried; baked in ovens; or poached in soups.

In cultures with a history of meat scarcity, meatballs were the food of celebrations and feasts, often well seasoned and further enriched with cheese, nuts, or fruit. In other cultures that historically had an abundance of meat over vegetables, meatballs were and are a usual, everyday meal. With good-quality meat, it is hard to go wrong, and by trying some new spices, you can bring the flavors of the whole world into your kitchen.

SPAIN

} # CHORIZO AND WHITE WINE TAPAS MEATBALLS

Yield: *43 small meatballs; 10 servings*

FOR THE MEATBALLS:

2 slices of bread, crusts removed
⅓ cup (80 ml) white wine
4 ounces (115 g) chorizo, uncooked sausage
1 pound (455 g) ground pork
1 egg
3 to 4 cloves of garlic, minced
2 tablespoons (8 g) fresh parsley
½ teaspoon paprika
1 teaspoon salt
¼ teaspoon black pepper

FOR SERVING:

Roasted red peppers
Olives

- Preheat the oven to 350°F (180°C, or gas mark 4). Grease a baking tray or line it with parchment paper.

- Soak the bread in a bowl with the white wine for 10 minutes. When it is very soggy, break it up with your hands into small pieces.

- Remove the chorizo from the casing and add it and the pork to the bowl. Add the egg, garlic, parsley, and seasonings to the meat. Mix with your hands, combining everything very well. With wet hands, roll neat little balls, about 1½ inches (3.8 cm) wide, that can be eaten in one bite. Place these on the prepared baking tray. They can be made ahead up to this point and kept in the fridge, ready to bake, for up to 1 day.

- Bake for 25 to 30 minutes until well browned and cooked through. A thermometer in the center should read 160°F (71°C).

- Serve warm or room temperature as tapas, alongside roasted red peppers and olives.

BRAZIL

} BULGUR AND LAMB MEATBALL SNACKS

Yield: *16 large meatballs; 4 servings*

1½ cups (355 ml) boiling water

1 cup (140 g) bulgur wheat

½ of a white onion

2 to 3 scallions

2 cloves of garlic

3 tablespoons (18 g) chopped fresh mint, or 2 teaspoons dried mint

1 pound (455 g) ground lamb or beef

¼ cup (60 ml) olive oil

1 teaspoon dried oregano

2 teaspoons salt

Pinch of cayenne pepper

Dash of hot sauce

About 2 cups (475 ml) oil, for frying

- Boil the water and pour it over the bulgur in a heatproof bowl. Leave to soak for 30 minutes.

- Mince the onion, scallions, garlic, and mint very small; this can be done quickly in a food processor. Combine this mixture in a bowl with the lamb, olive oil, oregano, salt, and spices. Measure 1½ cups (273 g) of the hydrated bulgur and add to the meat mixture. Knead it to combine everything well. This can be made up to a day ahead of cooking and kept covered in the refrigerator.

- Heat enough oil for deep-frying, to come about 2 inches (5 cm) up the sides of a high-sided pan. Heat to 350°F (180°C); a test piece should bubble vigorously when dropped in. While the oil is heating, form quenelles, football-shaped meatballs, by using 2 spoons or wet hands. Classic Brazilian kibe have pointed ends. Line them up on a waxed paper sheet until ready to fry. Fry the kibe in batches, not crowding the oil. Turn them while frying for even cooking. They should be done in the oil after 3 to 4 minutes. The outsides will be dark brown and crispy. Remove with a slotted spoon and drain on paper towels. Serve warm or room temperature.

Note:

Kibe is popular street food in Brazil. Eat it plain or serve with yogurt (see page 21). To make a gluten-free version of kibe, try using cooked quinoa or millet.

INDIA

NORTH INDIAN POTATO AND LAMB KOFTA

Yield: *30 medium meatballs; 6 servings*

1 pound (455 g) ground lamb
3 cups (675 g) cooked potatoes, roughly mashed
1 medium yellow onion, minced
2 teaspoons minced green chiles
3 cloves of garlic, pressed
1 egg
1 teaspoon salt
¼ teaspoon turmeric
¾ teaspoon ground coriander
¼ teaspoon ground cumin
⅓ cup (40 g) chickpea flour
1 to 2 tablespoons (15 to 28 ml) canola oil or ghee, for frying
Handful of chopped cilantro, for garnish

- Combine the lamb, potatoes, onion, chiles, garlic, egg, salt, and spices in a large bowl. Mix well with your hands, kneading until all the ingredients are well blended.

- With wet hands to avoid sticking, form 3-inch-long (7.5 cm), football-shaped meatballs with all the lamb, placing them on waxed paper to await cooking. Take up a portion of the meat mixture, roll it, and form the kofta oval shape by closing your fist over it several times. Soon it will turn into a rhythm, and they will all be rolled quickly.

- Pour the chickpea flour into a shallow dish or plate. Heat a frying pan with the oil over high heat. Roll each kofta in the chickpea flour, coat it all over, and shake off the excess. Place them in the hot oil. Don't crowd the pan; it will take 2 or 3 batches of frying. Fry for 8 to 10 minutes; as they brown, shake the pan so the kofta roll around and brown on all sides. Once toasted brown, remove to a foil-lined baking tray and finish cooking them all in the oven for about 10 minutes until a thermometer at the center reads 160°F (71°C).

- Serve warm with chopped cilantro.

Note:

The potato and meat combination is reminiscent of Indian samosas and shepherd's pie; it tastes of comfort.

MIDDLE EAST

} SESAME LAMB MEATBALLS

with Cucumber Mint Yogurt Dip

Yield: *40 small meatballs; 8 servings*

FOR THE YOGURT SAUCE:

1 cup (230 g) plain yogurt, cold
½ cup (70 g) grated cucumber
2 teaspoons dried mint or ¼ cup (24 g)
*   chopped fresh mint*
¼ teaspoon salt
Fresh ground black pepper

FOR THE MEATBALLS:

1 medium red onion, minced
1 tablespoon (15 ml) olive oil
½ to 1 cup (72 to 144 g) white sesame seeds
1 pound (455 g) ground lamb
2 cloves of garlic, minced
1 teaspoon salt
¼ teaspoon black pepper
1 teaspoon dried mint
½ teaspoon allspice
1 teaspoon ground cumin
1 egg
4 dried prunes, minced, or 4 tablespoons
*   (38 g) currants*
1 cup (115 g) bread crumbs
¼ cup (60 ml) water, or less

- Make the yogurt sauce. Mix the yogurt with the cucumber and mint. Adjust the seasonings to taste.

- Cook the onion with the olive oil for several minutes, just until softened.

- Lay the sesame seeds out in a bowl or plate. Line a baking tray with aluminum foil. There's no need to grease it. Preheat the oven to 450°F (230°C, or gas mark 8).

- Combine the ground meat with the cooked onion and all the following ingredients, adding half of the water. Mix the ingredients well. If the mixture is dense or dry, add more of the water. It should be moist but cohesive.

- Roll small, 1½-inch (3.8 cm) balls of the meat mixture. Roll each in the sesame seeds and then place on the baking tray. Bake in the preheated oven for 12 to 15 minutes. The sesame seeds will be toasted brown, and the fat drippings will have begun to bubble around the base of the balls. Remove the sesame balls to a serving platter with the yogurt sauce and eat while hot.

Tip:

These make an impressive appetizer. Place the yogurt sauce in a bowl alongside or drizzle some on top. Look for bags of sesame seeds in the international section of your market.

} PICNIC FAVORITE
SPICED FRIKKADELS

Yield: *22 large meatballs; 5 servings*

1 cup (115 g) unseasoned bread crumbs
½ cup (115 g) plain yogurt
1½ pounds (680 g) ground beef and pork, mixed
1 egg
2 cloves of garlic, minced
½ of an onion, minced
⅓ cup (5 g) chopped cilantro
1 teaspoon ground cumin
1 teaspoon coriander
½ teaspoon chili powder
1½ teaspoons salt
1 teaspoon black pepper
½ cup (60 g) chickpea flour
1 teaspoon turmeric
1 teaspoon paprika
*1 to 2 tablespoons (15 to 28 ml)
 safflower or canola oil*

* Combine the bread crumbs and yogurt in a bowl. Allow the mixture to rest for 5 minutes. Add the meat, egg, garlic, onion, cilantro, cumin, coriander, chili powder, salt, and pepper to the bread crumb mixture. Using your hands, squeeze the meat to incorporate the bread crumbs and onion.

* In a shallow dish, mix together the chickpea flour, turmeric, paprika, and a pinch of salt. Set aside.

* Preheat the oven to 350°F (180°C, or gas mark 4). Line a baking tray with aluminum foil. Heat a frying pan on medium high with the oil.

* Wet your hands to keep the meat from sticking. Form compact 2½-inch (6.4 cm) balls. Roll each in the seasoned chickpea flour, covering the surface. Place in the hot frying pan and cook the balls in batches on high to medium heat. Shake the pan often, to brown all over. Cook for about 5 minutes and remove to the prepared baking tray. Finish cooking through in the oven, 7 to 10 minutes. A meat thermometer should read 160°F (71°C) at the ball's interior.

* Serve warm or at room temperature.

CHINA

} LION'S HEAD MEATBALLS

Yield: *6 large meatballs; 6 servings*

FOR THE MEATBALLS:

1 large Napa or Chinese cabbage
1 pound (455 g) lean ground pork
2 tablespoons (28 ml) soy sauce, divided
2 scallions, sliced (divide white and green)
1 can (8 ounces, or 225 g) water chestnuts, drained and minced
1 tablespoon (15 ml) red rice wine or dry sherry
1 teaspoon salt
1 egg
3 cloves of garlic, minced
1 tablespoon (8 g) grated fresh ginger
Canola oil, for frying
4 whole dried Chinese mushrooms, or a handful of dried shiitake or porcini, soaked in warm water for 1 hour
1½ cups (355 ml) vegetable stock
½ cup (120 ml) water

FOR SERVING:

Cooked cellophane noodles or rice

- Slice the head of cabbage in half vertically. Cut each half into 3 wedges. Slice off the root ends. Lay the wedges into a high-sided, ovenproof serving dish, such as a casserole.

- In a large bowl, combine the pork, 1 tablespoon (15 ml) of the soy sauce, the white parts of the scallions, water chestnuts, rice wine, salt, egg, garlic, and ginger. Mix by hand until all the parts are just incorporated. With wet hands, form 6 large meatballs, about 3 inches (7.5 cm) across.

- Heat a skillet on high heat. Add enough canola oil to cover the bottom. When it is shimmering hot, place the meatballs in the skillet. Work to brown them on all sides, but do not cook through. Once they are browned, remove them to a serving dish. Create a cabbage nest for each special meatball.

- Preheat the oven to 300°F (150°C, or gas mark 2). Remove all but 2 tablespoons (28 ml) of the oil from the pan. Slice the mushrooms and add them to the oil. Fry for 1 minute. Add the vegetable stock, water, and remaining soy sauce. Scrape any brown bits from the pan into the sauce. Bring the sauce to a boil and then pour over the cabbage and meatballs.

- Check that the meatballs are secure in their cabbage nests, which look like a lion's mane once cooked. Cover the dish with foil or a lid. Braise the dish by cooking in a 300°F (150°C, or gas mark 2) oven for 20 minutes.

- Serve with cellophane noodles or rice.

Note:

Lion's head is a famous dish from the Shanghai region. The name *lion's head* describes the size of the meatball, which is large, because most other meatballs in China are small. The cabbage nest looks a little like a lion's mane. It is a popular dish with families and at banquets.

USA

} **ITALIAN WEDDING SOUP**

Yield: 30 small meatballs; 6 to 10 servings

FOR THE SOUP:

2 tablespoons (28 ml) olive oil

1 cup (160 g) finely diced onion

2 cloves of garlic, minced

⅓ cup (80 ml) white wine

4 cups (950 ml) chicken stock

4 cups (950 ml) water

2 cups (60 g) chopped Swiss chard
    or spinach (fresh or frozen)

1 cup (200 g) small pasta,
    such as stars (stelline)

Salt and black pepper, to taste

FOR THE MEATBALLS:

1 pound (455 g) ground pork
    (or half pork, half beef)

1 teaspoon salt

3 tablespoons (15 g) grated
    Parmigiano-Reggiano cheese

½ cup (60 g) bread crumbs

½ teaspoon garlic powder

1 egg

- In a large stockpot that will accommodate the soup, heat the olive oil, onion, and garlic on medium heat. After 5 to 6 minutes, when the onion is translucent and still pale in color, add the white wine. Boil the wine for 2 to 3 minutes to ensure the alcohol taste cooks off. When the volume of wine has reduced by around half, add the stock, water, and Swiss chard. Bring to a boil.

- While the soup is heating to a boil is an ideal time to make the meatballs. Mix the ground meat, salt, cheese, bread crumbs, garlic powder, and egg in a mixing bowl. Using 1 hand to hold the bowl steady, form the other hand into the shape of a claw and use it to mix, keeping the meat mixture light by turning it over and over with outstretched fingers, without kneading it. The ingredients should be incorporated but not a homogeneous mass. Using both hands, roll it into small 1-inch (2.5 cm) balls.

- Add the pasta to the lightly boiling soup and cook for about 6 minutes (follow package instructions) until tender. Add salt and pepper to taste. Turn the soup down to a low simmer and gently add the meatballs. Allow the meatballs to cook in the soup for 12 to 15 minutes. Refrain from stirring while the meatballs cook and keep the liquid at a low simmer. The balls are fragile until they are fully cooked. Test doneness by cutting one meatball in half; cook longer if necessary.

- Serve in soup bowls topped with grated cheese. This soup can be made ahead and reheats well.

Note:

Italian wedding soup is an Italian-American creation. Some people say it is called wedding soup because it "marries" pasta and meat in one soup.

JEWISH

DECONSTRUCTED RED KUBBEH SOUP WITH COUSCOUS

Yield: *25 medium meatballs; 6 to 8 servings*

FOR THE SOUP:

3 tablespoons (45 ml) olive oil

1 large red onion, sliced in wedges

1 large clove of garlic, sliced

3 carrots, roughly chopped

4 beets, peeled and sliced in wedges

4 tablespoons (64 g) tomato paste

4 cups (950 ml) chicken stock, or vegetable

4 cups (950 ml) water

1 teaspoon cumin seeds

½ teaspoon mustard powder

1 teaspoon paprika

Salt, to taste

1 lemon

FOR THE MEATBALLS:

6 cloves of garlic, minced

1 small onion, finely minced

1½ pounds (680 g) ground lamb or chicken

1½ teaspoons salt

FOR THE COUSCOUS:

4½ cups (1 L) boiling water

1 teaspoon salt

1 tablespoon (15 ml) olive oil

3 cups (525 g) couscous

Chopped parsley

* Heat the olive oil in a soup pot on high heat. Sauté the onion and garlic until soft. Add the carrots and beets and sauté briefly. Add the tomato paste and stir to cover all the vegetables. Sauté until the tomato paste is very fragrant and then add the chicken stock, water, and spices (reserving the lemon until the end of cooking). Bring the soup to a boil, turn it down to a low simmer, and work on the meatballs.

* To make the meatballs, combine the finely minced garlic and onion with the ground meat and salt. With wet hands, roll the mixture into neat compact balls, 2 to 3 inches (5 to 7.5 cm) wide. Lower the meatballs into the simmering soup. Cook on low for at least an hour.

* Meanwhile, make the couscous. In a wide pan with a lid, bring the water to a boil with the salt and olive oil. Turn off the heat. Stir in the couscous and put the lid on tightly. Let rest for 5 minutes, undisturbed. Before serving, fluff the couscous with a fork.

* After the soup is finished, take it off the heat and taste the soup. Add juice from half the lemon. Taste again, and if you like the sour notes, add more. There are wide ranges of preference about how sour this soup can be. Try bringing lemon slices to the table, and guests can adjust their own bowls. Serve with generous scoops of couscous on top of the soup and garnish with chopped parsley.

Tips:

Wear an apron while making this soup. Beets stain! Kept overnight in the fridge, the flavors develop further; it will be even better the next day.

Note:

Kubbeh soup is made in Jewish communities from Israel to Iraq to the United States. Traditionally, the meat and couscous are combined together as stuffed dumplings.

THAILAND

} EASY YELLOW CURRY WITH THAI MEATBALLS

Yield: 20 medium meatballs; 3 to 4 servings

FOR THE MEATBALLS:

1 pound (455 g) ground goat, beef, or lean pork

1 carrot, grated

¼ cup (25 g) chopped scallions

2 teaspoons grated fresh ginger

1 teaspoon salt

1½ tablespoons (12 g) tapioca starch or (18 g) potato starch

FOR THE CURRY:

2 tablespoons (28 ml) oil, canola or peanut

1 large onion, sliced thin

¼ cup (60 g) yellow curry paste

1 can (14 ounces, or 390 g) coconut milk, full fat

2 teaspoons palm sugar

½ tablespoon (7 ml) fish sauce

2 kaffir lime leaves

2 tablespoons (28 ml) lime juice

OPTIONAL ADDITIONS:

Add with the onions: diced potatoes, eggplant, zucchini, squash, cauliflower, or bell pepper

Add with the coconut milk: chard, spinach, snow peas, green peas, or green beans

Add when serving: bean sprouts, chopped roasted unsalted peanuts, chopped cilantro, mint, basil, or hot sauce

Serve on rice or wide rice noodles.

* Combine the ground meat with all the other meatball ingredients. Using your hands, thoroughly infuse the flavors into the meat by squeezing the meat through your fingers several times. If you use wet hands, the meat will not stick to your hands. Roll the meat mixture into bite-size balls, about 1 inch (2.5 cm) across.

* Heat the oil in a wok or soup pot. Cook the meatballs on high heat so that the outsides brown. Remove from the pot and set aside; they need not be cooked fully at this point.

* Add the sliced onion into the same oil. Cook on medium heat for about 5 minutes. Add the curry paste, stir, and allow it to sizzle for 30 seconds. This develops the herbal flavors. Pour in the coconut milk, stirring to combine. Add the sugar, fish sauce, lime leaves, and lime juice. Return the meatballs and any collected juices to the sauce. Simmer on low for about 20 minutes. If the sauce becomes too thick, add some stock or water to thin it.

* Serve hot over rice or noodles. It is a nice touch to allow diners to select their own toppings. Put all the herbs and bean sprouts on the table, and people can customize their curry.

Note:

This curry is so quick to whip up, you may find yourself making it for dinner all the time. Don't feel bad about "cheating" with a store-bought paste. Yellow curry paste is more complex than either red or green curry, and even in Thailand, it is more often purchased than made within the home! To extend the sauce, add broth or water. Or turn it into a soup by adding several cups (1.4 to 1.6 L) of water or vegetable stock and another can of coconut milk. The recipe is very forgiving and one of my most reliable recipes for company. It makes everybody happy, without dairy and gluten, and you can replace the meatballs with fish or even tofu. Make it your own.

CAMBODIA

LEMONGRASS PORK MEATBALL SOUP

Yield: *24 small meatballs; 4 servings*

FOR THE MEATBALLS:

1 pound (455 g) lean ground pork
½ teaspoon palm sugar
1 teaspoon salt
1 teaspoon chili paste
1 tablespoon (15 ml) fish sauce
1 tablespoon (15 ml) lime juice
1½ teaspoons tapioca or potato starch

FOR THE SOUP:

4 tablespoons (60 g) tamarind paste or fruit (see Tip)
1 cup (235 ml) warm water
2 stalks of lemongrass
6 cloves of garlic, peeled
1 inch (2.5 cm) piece of fresh ginger, peeled
1 large shallot
3 kefir lime leaves
4⅔ cups (1.1 L) water, divided
2 tablespoons (28 ml) fish sauce
1½ tablespoons (27 g) salt
1 tablespoon (12 g) palm sugar
1 pound (455 g) watercress or arugula

* Mix the ground pork with the sugar, salt, chili paste, fish sauce, lime juice, and starch. The starch will help bind the meatballs. Use cornstarch if you cannot find tapioca or potato starch. Use your hands to combine them well, squeezing the meat through your fingers several times. Roll into bite-size balls, about 1 inch (2.5 cm) across, and place them onto a plate or waxed paper to await cooking. Use wet hands when rolling the balls to prevent the meat from sticking.

* Submerge the tamarind paste or fruit in the warm water. Allow it to steep 5 to 10 minutes. The paste should dissolve. If you are using fresh or dried fruits, scoop them out of the water, put into a little strainer, and press them with your finger or a spoon to press the soft fruit pulp back into the water. Discard the hard seeds and fibers.

* To make the soup base, trim the top and bottom of the lemongrass, remove the toughest outside leaves, and chop into smaller lengths. Put all of the lemongrass, garlic, ginger, shallot, and lime leaves, and ⅔ cup (160 ml) of water, into a blender, food processor, or mortar and pestle. Blend until smooth.

* Transfer the lemongrass paste to a soup pot. Cook over medium heat for about 6 minutes, stirring frequently. This really brings out the flavors from the herbs. Add the 4 cups (950 ml) of water, fish sauce, salt, and palm sugar. Bring the broth to a simmer. Add the meatballs and simmer for 30 to 40 minutes. Take off the heat and stir in the watercress and tamarind water. You may want to add half of the tamarind water at first and taste it, if you are wary of tangy flavors. Serve in bowls with chili sauce.

Tip:

Tamarind is a fruit, sold mostly in a paste or a whole dried form. It is described as sour, but it is in actuality more tangy, with a background of fruity sweetness. If you cannot find tamarind, use ⅓ cup (80 ml) lime juice instead. For a shortcut, use 1 to 2 tablespoons (16 to 32 g) of Thai green curry paste in place of the flavor paste.

COSTA RICA

} SOPA DE ALBONDIGAS

Yield: *24 small meatballs; 5 servings*

FOR THE SOUP:

4 to 6 cups (950 ml to 1.4 L) beef broth, homemade or good quality

2 cups (475 ml) water

2 onions, minced

1 celery stalk, minced

2 cloves of garlic, minced

1 teaspoon dried oregano

½ teaspoon dried marjoram

½ of a green serrano chile, sliced very thin

Salt, to taste

2 ripe, yellow plantains (See Tip.)

Cilantro, optional

FOR THE MEATBALLS:

2 slices of bread

1 small yellow onion, minced

½ pound (225 g) ground pork

½ teaspoon salt

¼ teaspoon ground cumin

¼ teaspoon chili powder

* Pour the broth and water into a soup pot. Heat on high. The onion, celery, and garlic can be minced by hand or in the food processor. Put the vegetables into the boiling broth, along with the herbs and salt. Since heat in chile peppers varies greatly, it is wise to add a small amount, allow it to cook, taste, and add more if desired. Turn the heat down, cook the soup at a simmer, and make the meatballs.

* Rinse the bread, soaking it in water, and place it in the bottom of a bowl. Add the onion, ground pork, salt, and spices. Using your hands, squeeze the mixture so it squishes out between your fingers. Mix like this until the meat and onions are well mixed and stuck with each other. Roll into small 1-inch (2.5 cm) balls, dropping them into the simmering soup as each one is formed. Add more beef stock or water if necessary to cover the meatballs.

* Cook the soup at a simmer for at least 30 minutes. Before serving, slice the ripe plantain into bite-size pieces and add to the soup. Allow the plantain to simmer for 10 minutes within the soup.

* Serve as is in soup bowls or with fresh cilantro sprinkled on top.

Tip:

Plantains are a staple food in nearly all tropical parts of the globe. A cousin of the banana, they are eaten cooked, in all stages of ripeness. When green, they are hard and may be fried and cooked like a potato. When black and very sweet, plantains are cooked like fruit.

WEST AFRICA

} # SPICED MEATBALL, YAM, AND PEANUT STEW OVER COUSCOUS

Yield: *14 medium meatballs; 3 to 4 servings*

FOR THE MEATBALLS:

1 pound (455 g) ground beef
1 egg
1 teaspoon salt
¾ teaspoon chili powder
½ teaspoon ground ginger
½ teaspoon ground cinnamon
¼ teaspoon ground cloves

FOR THE STEW:

2 tablespoons (28 ml) peanut or canola oil
2 medium onions, diced
2 cloves of garlic, minced
5 or 6 plum tomatoes, chopped
4 cups (950 ml) water
2 yams or sweet potatoes, peeled and diced
2 handfuls of shelled unsalted peanuts
½ cup (130 g) chunky natural peanut butter
Salt and black pepper, to taste

FOR SERVING:

Couscous (see page 27)

* To make the meatballs, mix the ground beef with the egg and all the seasonings. Mix them by hand until everything is well combined. Using wet hands so the meat does not stick, roll 2-inch (5 cm) balls of the mixture. Set onto a plate.

* Heat a stew pot over medium-high heat and add a little of the oil. Cook the meatballs in batches to brown the outsides. Don't worry about cooking them through at this stage. Once browned, remove to a plate. Repeat with all the meatballs.

* Add a little more oil to the pan if necessary and cook the diced onion with a big pinch of salt on medium heat until very soft, about 7 minutes. Add the garlic and cook for another minute. Add the tomatoes and all their juices. Stir to meld the onion and tomato flavors. After about 3 minutes of cooking, pour in the water, scraping the bottom of the pan to loosen any onion stuck there.

* Return the meatballs to the stew, along with the diced yam and peanuts. Add more water or tomatoes if necessary to keep everything covered. Keep the stew at a simmer for an hour as the flavors meld and everything becomes tender. The broth will reduce a little bit and thicken more. This stew is even better the following day.

* Toward the end of its cooking, stir in the chunky peanut butter so it melts into the stew and add salt and pepper to taste. Simmer another few minutes so the peanut butter really melts in.

* Ladle over tender couscous or for something different, try cooked millet or quinoa.

Note:

Groundnut (peanut) stews are a signature of West African cuisine, sometimes with meat and often with vegetables. Try squash or pumpkin as a substitution; they make a hearty meal. There are very few rules to a stew like this. Throw in what fancies you and just let it all simmer down!

USA

LOUISIANA ALLIGATOR MEATBALL GUMBO

Yield: 30 small meatballs; 8 to 10 servings

FOR THE MEATBALLS:

1 pound (455 g) ground alligator, rabbit, or chicken

1 egg

1 teaspoon onion powder

¾ teaspoon garlic powder

¼ cup (30 g) bread crumbs

1 teaspoon salt

½ teaspoon black pepper

About ⅓ cup (42 g) all-purpose flour, to coat

2 to 3 tablespoons (28 to 45 ml) oil for frying

FOR THE GUMBO:

1 pound (455 g) smoked sausage,
    Polish or garlic, sliced thin

2 cups (320 g) chopped onion

⅔ cup (100 g) chopped green bell peppers

½ cup (50 g) chopped scallions, green part only

1 tablespoon (10 g) minced garlic

⅔ cup (160 ml) corn or vegetable oil

⅔ cup (83 g) all-purpose flour

2 quarts (1.9 L) cold water

2 teaspoons salt

1 teaspoon black pepper

⅛ teaspoon cayenne pepper

½ teaspoon hot sauce

1½ teaspoons thyme

2 bay leaves

2 pounds (900 g) shrimp, deveined

2 to 3 tablespoons (14 to 21 g) filé powder

FOR SERVING:

Cooked long-grain rice

• For the meatballs, combine the ground meat with the egg, onion and garlic powders, bread crumbs, salt, and pepper. Roll into bite-size balls. Roll each one in flour before frying. Heat the oil in a cast-iron skillet. When it is shimmering hot, add the meatballs, not crowding the pan. Sear on all sides. It is not necessary for them to be cooked through at this point. Remove them and set aside. Repeat with all the meatballs.

• In a large, heavy-bottomed pot, cook the sausage on low until the fat begins to melt out. Add the chopped onion, bell peppers, scallions, and garlic. Toss everything to coat. Cover with a lid and cook for 10 minutes to soften the vegetables. Check once or twice to make sure nothing is sticking to the bottom.

• Make the roux. Put the oil in a small pot. Stir in the flour with a wooden spoon. Cook the roux on medium-low heat; it will take about 20 or 30 minutes to achieve the desired color. Stir to move the more toasted roux into the lighter areas. It will darken very slowly, all the way to a nutty brown, the color of dark brown sugar. Once browned, remove it from the heat. A burnt roux is terribly bitter and cannot be used in gumbo, so avoid having to repeat the process. Immediately scoop the roux out of the small pan and stir it into the softened vegetables so it will stop cooking.

• Stir the roux and vegetables until well coated. Add a small portion of the water and stir, making a paste. Add the remaining water and seasonings (except the filé powder) to the pot. Bring to a boil and lower the heat to a simmer. Add the meatballs. Simmer for 1 hour. Stir in the shrimp and simmer for about 7 more minutes. Turn off the heat and wait for all simmering activity to end. Stir in the filé powder and let it rest 5 minutes to thicken. Serve in bowls with fluffy long-grain rice.

Note:

Gumbo is a true melting pot resulting from the cooking traditions of the early Americas, West Africa, and France. Gumbo is a stew with a roux to give it texture and smoky flavor. Filé powder thickens the stew and was used for ages by the native Choctaw people in the southeastern United States.

MONGOLIA

} **MEATBALL CHOWDER**

Yield: *35 small meatballs; 4 servings*

1 tablespoon (14 g) butter
1 large pinch of salt
1 large onion, diced
1½ pounds (680 g) ground goat, mutton, or beef
½ cup (60 g) cracker or bread crumbs
1 egg
1½ teaspoons salt
½ teaspoon black pepper
4 cups (950 ml) milk, goat, or cow
1 pound (455 g) potato, small dice
Fresh ground pepper

* Cook the butter, salt, and diced onion in a soup pot for nearly 10 minutes on low heat until very soft.

* Meanwhile, mix the ground meat with the cracker crumbs, egg, salt, and pepper. Mix very well and roll into small, bite-size balls. Place the meatballs atop the softened onions and cover the pot with a lid for about 5 minutes. This steams the meatballs. Keep the heat low so the bottom doesn't scorch.

* Add the milk, stirring carefully to avoid crushing any meatballs. Scrape any onions off the bottom of the pot. Add in the potatoes and season with pepper. Bring the chowder just to a boil and then simmer on low for 15 to 20 minutes. When finished, the meatballs should be cooked through and the potatoes fork tender. Serve hot in bowls with fresh ground pepper.

FRANCE }

CASSOULET WITH DUCK CONFIT AND PORK MEATBALLS

Yield: 28 small meatballs; 8 to 10 servings

FOR THE BEANS:

2 cups (384 g) dry white beans (Great Northern or flageolet)

½ of an onion

½ pound (225 g) bacon, thick cut

Bouquet garni herbs, tied together (1 bay leaf, 1 sprig of parsley, 1 sprig of thyme, and 1 sprig of sage)

FOR THE SAUCE:

1 medium onion, chopped

2 cloves of garlic, minced

1 cup (235 ml) white wine

1 tablespoon (16 g) tomato paste

Salt and black pepper

FOR THE MEATBALLS:

2 slices of dry bread, crusts removed

⅓ cup (80 ml) milk

1 pound (455 g) ground pork

1 medium onion, grated

2 tablespoons (8 g) chopped parsley

2 egg yolks

1 teaspoon salt

Black pepper

FOR THE CASSOULET:

Duck confit, 6 legs or 1 whole duck

2 cups (230 g) plain coarse bread crumbs

SERVING SUGGESTION:

Green salad

- Place the dry beans in a bowl covered with plenty of cool water. Soak overnight.

- Drain the water the beans were soaking in. Place the beans in a big pot and cover with about 4 liters (4 quarts) of water, the onion, bacon, and bouquet garni. Bring to a boil and skim off any foam. Turn down to low heat and simmer for about 1 hour until the beans are tender and cooked through. Keep the beans in the liquid. When ready to assemble the cassoulet, strain the beans and keep the liquid. Discard the cooked onion and the bouquet garni.

- Remove the bacon from the beans and chop into bite-size pieces.

- Chop the confit of duck into portions. If using whole legs, cut into two pieces (1 drumstick, 1 thigh). If it is a whole duck, cut it into 8 pieces, as you would a chicken. In a sauté pan on high, brown the skin lightly. Remove and set aside.

- Make the pork meatballs. Soak the bread and milk in a bowl for about 10 minutes. Break up the bread with your fingers until it is all in small pieces. Combine the ground pork, onion, and parsley. Add the soaked bread, egg yolks, salt, and pepper and mix. Form into small 1-inch (2.5 cm) balls, rolling them with wet hands to keep the meat from sticking. Heat a bit of olive oil in a sauté pan with 2-inch-high (5 cm) sides. Sauté the meatballs, browning on all sides. Turn down the heat, cook all the way through, and remove from the pan.

- Make the sauce. There should be about 2 tablespoons (28 ml) of oil remaining in the meatball pan. If there is more, set it aside; if there is less, add some olive oil. Add the chopped onion. Cook, stirring once in a while. In about 5 minutes, the onion will be soft. Then add the garlic and cook for 1 minute. Add the white wine to deglaze the pan. Let it cook 2 minutes and scrape all brown bits off the bottom. Add the tomato paste. Season well with salt and pepper and simmer for 4 to 5 minutes before taking off the heat.

- Now It's time to assemble the cassoulet! To fit it all in one, you need a large (8 quart [7.6 L]) casserole dish or wide Dutch oven, with 5- or 6-inch-tall (13 or 15 cm) sides. Place one-third of the beans on the bottom of the casserole dish. Cover the layer of beans with the meatballs. Spoon half of the wine sauce over. Place another one-third of the beans on top of the meatballs. Make the next layer of duck confit. Spoon the remaining wine sauce over the duck. Cover the duck with the remaining beans. Place the bacon on top of the beans. It is very important to taste the liquid the beans cooked in. It should be like a soup, with enough salt and pepper, so add more if needed. Carefully pour this bean liquid over the cassoulet, filling it just to the top of the beans, no more. Cover the top with the bread crumbs.

- To make individual portions, which are elegant for dinner parties, fill high-sided oven-safe dishes with the same method described above. Depending on the size of the dish, you may decide to remove the middle layer of beans.

- Bake in a preheated 350°F (180°C, or gas mark 4) oven for a total of 1 hour and 15 minutes. After the first 20 minutes of cooking, check on the cassoulet. The bread crumbs should have toasted. Use a spoon to crack it in many places and allow the liquid to come up into the crust. Do this once or twice again throughout the following hour. This method creates a moist, crunchy crust instead of a dry one. If the crust begins to brown too much, turn the heat down or drizzle any leftover meat fat or bean juice over top.

- Serve the cassoulet hot, right out of the oven, alongside a green salad and a robust red wine for a classic comforting French feast.

Tip:

Assemble the cassoulet up to a day ahead, filling the casserole with bean liquid. Do not add the bread crumbs until ready to cook. Cover and keep in the fridge up to 1 day. Baking may take 15 minutes longer.

USA

} CAJUN MEATBALL STEW

Yield: *35 medium meatballs; 5 servings*

FOR THE MEATBALLS:

½ cup (120 ml) peanut oil (or canola)
1 pound (455 g) ground beef
½ pound (225 g) ground pork butt
1 egg
½ cup (60 g) dry plain bread crumbs
2 tablespoons (28 ml) Worcestershire sauce
2 teaspoons garlic powder
½ teaspoon cayenne pepper
½ teaspoon paprika
1 teaspoon dried thyme
1 teaspoon ground black pepper
1½ teaspoons salt

FOR THE GRAVY:

5 tablespoons (39 g) all-purpose flour
1 cup (160 g) diced onion
1 cup (150 g) diced green bell pepper
1 cup (120 g) diced celery
1½ cups (355 ml) water

- To make the meatballs, preheat the oven to 375°F (190°C, or gas mark 5).

- Pour the oil into the bottom of a 6-quart (5.7 L) Dutch oven or a large ovenproof skillet with high sides.

- Combine the ground meat, egg, bread crumbs, Worcestershire sauce, spices, and salt in a bowl. Using your hand in the shape of a claw, mix the meatball ingredients. Use your fingers to scoop under the meat and lift and turn. Continue mixing with this gentle claw-scooping motion until everything is mixed up. It will still be lumpy and the bread crumbs will still appear separate from the meat. Roll the mixture into compact 1½-inch (3.8 cm) balls. Place them in the oiled Dutch oven in a single layer.

- Cook in the preheated oven for 45 minutes. Refrain from shaking the pan or stirring the meatballs for the entire cooking time. If the pan is well oiled, they will release from the bottom all on their own. In this way, they are both roasted and fried; when done, the meatballs have a dark brown, crunchy crust with lots of flavor.

- Remove the Dutch oven to the stovetop.

- To make the gravy, use a slotted spoon to remove the meatballs to a plate. Carefully pour the hot oil into a glass measuring cup.

- Return ⅓ cup (80 ml) of the oil to the Dutch oven, along with the flour. Scrape all brown bits free from the bottom of the pan; a wooden spoon with a flat edge is the best tool for this. Turn the heat on medium to cook the roux. Stand by the pan and continue to scrape the bottom with the wooden spoon. The slurry of white flour and oil will soon begin to boil and darken in color. First it will turn golden, then toasted brown, and finally dark brown. This can take 7 to 10 minutes, depending on your stove. Near the finish it tends to darken very quickly. Pay close attention, as burnt roux is bitter. When you have attained the desired dark brown color, toss in the diced vegetables all at once. This stops the cooking of the roux.

- Stir a few times to coat the vegetables. Cook the vegetables on medium heat for 10 minutes, stirring occasionally. The vegetables will soften and become tender. The roux will clump up and appear crunchy. Don't allow it to burn or take on any more color.

- Pour the water into the pan, slowly, stirring to make a smooth sauce. Turn up the heat to high to bring it to a full boil before turning the heat down low to a simmer. Place all the meatballs into the gravy. Simmer, partially covered, on the lowest setting for 1 hour.

} BACON AND ONION MEATBALL SLIDERS

Yield: *15 large meatballs; 5 servings*

1 package (1 pound, or 455 g) bacon, thin/regular cut

2 pounds (900 g) ground beef, chuck

1½ teaspoons salt

Generous amount of black pepper

Dash of Worcestershire sauce

Sliced American or Cheddar cheese

3 large sweet white onions, sliced

15 dinner rolls (Soft potato bread works the best.)

Long toothpicks, to keep the sliders upright

* Cut the bacon into half lengths. You can slice right through a package with kitchen shears or take a knife to the whole pile. Set aside 1 rasher of bacon to cook with the onions. Preheat the oven to 400°F (200°C, or gas mark 6). Prepare the 2 halves of a broiler tray or arrange a metal cooling rack (the type used for cookies) atop a baking tray with edges. The idea is to elevate the meatballs while cooking so that the bacon fat will drip down into the pan below.

* Season the beef with salt, pepper, and Worcestershire sauce. Mix up well. When it's all combined, roll into compact 2½-inch (6.3 cm) balls. Wrap each ball with a strip of bacon. Place the bacon-wrapped meatballs down on the broiler tray, with the two overlapping ends of the bacon on the bottom.

* Cook in the 400°F (200°C, or gas mark 6) oven for about 20 minutes. The bacon will be sizzling, cooked, and crispy. The meatball inside will be cooked. Remove the tray from the oven and lay a slice of cheese atop each one. If your cheese is on the thicker side, pop the tray back into the oven for just 30 seconds until the cheese melts. Remove the tray.

* While the meatballs are baking, cook the onions. In a large, well-seasoned cast-iron pan, cook the reserved rasher of bacon (or 2 cut strips) and all the sliced onions on high heat. This ends up as delicious bacon-tasting onions. Stir occasionally. When all the onions are soft, keep them warm until the sliders are ready.

* Cut the buns or rolls in half, so there is a top and a bottom. Arrange the bottoms on a large platter, one for each meatball. When the meatballs with cheese come out of the oven, place one in each bun. Lay the onions on and then the top of the bun. This can be a messy assembly, but that is part of the fun. Pin everything in place with long toothpicks. Serve with the usual condiments: mustard, ketchup, and pickles.

LAOS

PORK MEATBALLS IN LETTUCE CUPS

with Chili Dipping Sauce

Yield: *30 small meatballs; 4 servings*

FOR THE MEATBALLS:

1 dried tamarind pod (See Tip on page 30.)
⅓ cup (80 ml) water
1½ pounds (680 g) ground pork
1 teaspoon salt
1 tablespoon (15 ml) safflower oil
3 shallots, minced
5 cloves of garlic, minced
1 tablespoon (12 g) palm sugar, or sugar in the raw
1 tablespoon (6 g) minced fresh ginger
2½ tablespoons (40 ml) fish sauce

FOR THE CHILI SAUCE:

6 cherry tomatoes, or 1 tablespoon (16 g)
*   sun-dried tomato paste*
1 tablespoon (6 g) sliced scallions
1 tablespoon (15 g) chili paste, such as Sriracha
2½ tablespoons (40 ml) soy sauce

FOR SERVING THE LETTUCE CUPS:

Lettuce leaves, such as Boston or Bibb lettuce,
*   washed and dried*
Scallions, chopped
Cilantro, chopped
Basil, chopped
Lime wedges
Shredded carrots or thin slices of cucumber
Cooked white rice

* To make the tamarind water, crack the shell off the tamarind and place 4 of the pulp-covered seeds into the ⅓ cup (80 ml) water. After 5 to 10 minutes, the fruit pulp looks pale and hydrated. Pour the water and pulp through a fine strainer into another bowl. Press the pulp through the strainer and add it to the water. Discard the hard tamarind seeds. If you are able to find tamarind paste, soak 1 tablespoon (16 g) in water.

* Mix the pork with the salt. Using wet hands to stop the meat from sticking, form small 1-inch (2.5 cm) balls with all of the pork.

* Place a wok over high heat. When hot, pour the safflower oil down the side so it heats up. Toss in the pork balls, using a spoon or spatula to stir-fry them in the oil, meaning, keep them continuously and rapidly moving. When the balls have changed color from pink to white, and are beginning to turn golden brown, add the shallots and garlic. Stir-fry for 1 to 2 minutes, looking for when the shallots and garlic turn golden brown. When this happens, add the sugar, ginger, and fish sauce. Stir well to combine everything. The sauce will bubble vigorously. Turn down the heat to medium low and cook for about 4 minutes, just until the pork balls are cooked through. They will have much more resistance when pressed with a spoon. As the fish sauce cooks, it can have a stinky odor. Remember, it tastes much better than the smell of it cooking!

* To make the chili sauce, put a small nonstick skillet on medium heat. Place the cherry tomatoes in the skillet. As they blister and blacken in spots, shake them around. When plump and roasted, remove to a bowl. Smash the tomatoes and scallions with a muddler or pestle to bring their flavors together. Add the chili paste and soy sauce. Taste and adjust the seasonings. (If you have sun-dried tomato paste, there is no need to roast and smash the tomatoes.)

* Serve the fixings for the lettuce leaves in separate bowls or piles on a platter, so guests can assemble their own lettuce cups. Rice is nice served alongside the lettuce cups. This is a great meal for a dinner party; everyone passing the dishes back and forth is a lot of fun.

} BÁHN MI MEATBALL SANDWICH ON BAGUETTE

Yield: *20 medium meatballs; 4 servings*

FOR THE QUICK CARROT PICKLES:

½ cup (100 g) sugar
½ teaspoon salt
½ cup (120 ml) water
¾ cup (175 ml) white vinegar
2 to 3 carrots, peeled and cut in thick matchsticks

FOR THE MEATBALLS:

1 pound (455 g) ground pork
2 cloves of garlic, minced
1 teaspoon salt *— use a lot*
1 teaspoon black pepper *less*
1 to 2 tablespoons (8 to 16 g) grated fresh ginger
1 tablespoon (15 ml) fish sauce
1 tablespoon (20 g) chili sauce
1 tablespoon (12 g) sugar, preferably palm
1 tablespoon (8 g) cornstarch

FOR EACH SANDWICH:

Baguette bread, about 7 inches (18 cm) (See Note.)
Pâté
Mayonnaise
3 cucumber strips, very thin
Strips of pickled carrot
Cilantro, chopped
Drizzle of soy sauce
Drizzle of red chili sauce

- Make the carrot pickles 30 minutes ahead of time or up to 4 days ahead. Stir the sugar and salt into the water and vinegar until dissolved. Add the carrots. Cover them and set aside for at least 30 minutes to absorb the flavors. The pickled carrots offer a bright acidic crunch that highlights the meaty, fatty flavors of the pâté and meatballs. They are too good to be skipped.

- Preheat the oven to 400°F (200°C, or gas mark 6). Prepare a baking tray to fit all the meatballs. In a large mixing bowl, combine the pork and all the meatball ingredients. Using your hands, knead it all together, incorporating the flavors. Roll into compact 1½-inch (3.8 cm) balls and place them onto the baking tray. If you use wet hands, the meat won't be sticky. There should be around 20 meatballs. Bake in the preheated oven for 15 to 20 minutes until cooked through. Slice one open to check the color.

- Slit the bread lengthwise. If your bread is not super soft, dig out some of the bread from the inside of the top half so that there is about ½ inch (1.3 cm) remaining and the meatballs will nestle into the sandwich. (You can use this bread for crumbs in other recipes.)

- Spread a generous amount of pâté on one cut side of the bread. Spread mayonnaise on the other. Lay cucumbers and pickled carrots onto the sandwich. Top with several meatballs and cilantro. Drizzle as much soy sauce and chili sauce as you like. Place the top on the sandwich and dig in.

Note:

Báhn mi sandwiches are a fusion of Vietnamese and French cuisine. During the French colonial period in Vietnam, the baguette was introduced and has remained popular. The crust on Vietnamese baguettes is softer than true French baguettes. This recipe is a basic báhn mi, meant to be elaborated upon. Add to the spicy, sour, crunchy, luscious meatiness of this sandwich with sausages, pork belly, slices of roast pork, cured meats, grilled tofu, radish, onions, or green beans. There are no rules!

MOROCCO

} # PITA SANDWICHES

with Lamb Kefta, Harissa, and Chopped Salad

Yield: *30 small meatballs; 6 servings*

FOR THE KEFTA:

1½ pounds (680 g) ground lamb
2 onions, grated
2 tablespoons (12 g) chopped fresh mint
2 tablespoons (2 g) chopped fresh cilantro
1 teaspoon ground cumin
1 teaspoon ground coriander
Pinch of nutmeg
Fresh ground black pepper
1½ teaspoons salt

FOR THE CHOPPED SALAD:

1 cucumber, seeded and diced
1 tomato, seeded and diced
1 clove of garlic, smashed
½ cup (115 g) plain yogurt
Juice from ½ of a lemon
Pinch of salt

FOR SERVING:

Harissa paste
Olive oil
Pita bread

- Mix together the meat, onions, herbs, and spices. Knead and squeeze the mixture through your fingers, developing a cohesive meat paste. Form into small 1-inch (2.5 cm) balls. These can be speared onto skewers to grill, which takes about 5 minutes. If you are to cook them indoors, use a hot broiler. Line a baking tray with aluminum foil, put the balls onto the prepared pan, cook under the broiler for 5 to 8 minutes, and shake around a few times to get color on all sides.

- Mix up the chopped salad, thoroughly stirring together the yogurt and vegetables. Add salt to your own taste.

- Harissa is a thick chili paste. Mix a little of it with some olive oil to thin it out enough to drizzle it in a sandwich.

- Cut a pita bread in half and stuff it with a few kefta, a drizzle of harissa, and plenty of chopped salad.

DENMARK

} # OPEN-FACED MEATBALL SANDWICH

Frikadeller Smørrebrød

Yield: *20 medium meatballs; 8 to 10 servings*

FOR THE FRIKADELLER:

6 ounces (170 g) ground lean pork
6 ounces (170 g) ground veal or beef
1 cup (160 g) grated onion
1 egg
¾ teaspoon salt
3 tablespoons (23 g) all-purpose flour
¼ cup (30 g) bread crumbs
Fresh ground black pepper
¼ teaspoon allspice
½ to ¾ cup (120 to 175 ml) soda water
1 tablespoon (14 g) butter

FOR THE SMØRREBRØD:

Dark rye bread, dense and thinly sliced
Mustard
Fresh dill
Fresh or pickled cucumbers
Fresh pepper

SERVING SUGGESTIONS:

Boiled potatoes
Gravy
Cooked cabbage

- In a mixing bowl, mix the ground meats with the grated onion, egg, salt, flour, bread crumbs, pepper, and allspice. Mix it up gently by hand and add the soda water. It will fizz. It is a loose mixture; don't worry about rolling it into balls.

- Melt the butter in a cast-iron frying pan on high heat. Using a soup spoon or tablespoon, take a spoonful of the frikadeller mixture and lay it into the hot butter. Continue until the frying pan is full but not crowded. Try to lay them in neat egg shapes. Use 2 spoons if this helps. The oil may spit a little bit. They are ready to flip over when the edges firm up and you can see the meat cooking up the sides of the patty. Fry about 3 minutes on each side, more if necessary.

- To make the smørrebrød, spread mustard on 1 slice of rye bread and top with dill, frikadeller, and pickled cucumbers. It is a point of pride in Denmark to create beautiful smørrebrød, like small edible pieces of modern art. So let your creativity fly. For a classic Danish supper, serve frikadeller with boiled potatoes, gravy, and cabbage.

Note:

Frikadeller is the national dish of Denmark. They range from thin patties to patties that approach a ball shape. There tend to be many small variations on the basic ingredients, as each family and restaurant has its own best version. They are indeed comfort food and will be loved by all, as they are simple and flavorful.

USA

} MELTING MESSY MEATBALL SUB

Yield: *25 large meatballs; 3 to 4 servings*

FOR THE RED SAUCE:

2 tablespoons (28 ml) olive oil
2 large onions, diced small
1 teaspoon salt
½ teaspoon black pepper
1 can (28 ounces, or 785 g) crushed tomatoes
1 tablespoon (16 g) tomato paste
½ cup (120 ml) water
1½ teaspoons dried oregano
1 teaspoon garlic powder
½ teaspoon sugar

FOR THE MEATBALLS:

1 pound (455 g) lean ground beef
¼ pound (115 g) ground pork
1 teaspoon salt
1 egg
½ cup (60 g) bread crumbs
⅓ cup (80 ml) milk
½ teaspoon garlic powder
2 tablespoons (8 g) chopped parsley
2 teaspoons dried oregano
Pinch of red pepper flakes

FOR THE SUB ASSEMBLY:

Sub rolls
Provolone cheese slices

- For the red sauce, heat the olive oil and diced onions on medium heat in a very large saucepan or Dutch oven. Add the salt and pepper, cooking the onions for about 5 minutes until wilted and soft. Remove ¼ cup (65 g) of the cooked onions to add to the meatballs. Add the tomatoes, tomato paste, water, oregano, garlic, and sugar. Stir once in a while, simmer on low for about 10 minutes, and then remove from the heat and set aside.

- In a large mixing bowl, combine the ¼ cup (65 g) cooked onion reserved from the sauce making with the ground meats and all other meatball ingredients. Mix it with your hands, keeping things light by scooping up the meat and letting it fall through your fingers again and again. This way, it gets mixed but not compacted or kneaded, avoiding a dense meatball result.

- Preheat the oven to 400°F (200°C, or gas mark 6). Rinse your hands in cold water to prevent the meatballs from sticking while rolling them. Form neat, golf-ball-size meatballs, lining them up on a baking tray. Bake in the oven for about 15 minutes until just cooked through. Remove from the oven and dump the meatballs into the sauce. Keep the sauce and meatballs hot while making the sandwiches.

- Take your sub rolls and slit them lengthwise, leaving 1 crusty side attached so it opens like a book. Line them up, open like books, on a baking tray. In each sandwich, put 3 slices of provolone cheese; they will overlap a little. Put the tray under a hot broiler so the cheese melts. Remove from the broiler. Scoop several meatballs onto each sub, lining them up on top of the melted cheese. Top with extra sauce for a sloppy sub. Close the sandwiches up as much as possible. Eat while hot and still melty.

Note:

The sub sandwich originates in the early 20th century in Italian American communities. They were sold all over the northeast states, from Pennsylvania to Maine, in pizza shops, which is still the case today.

} MEATBALLS WITH TOMATO SAUCE

Yield: *45 small meatballs; 7 servings*

FOR THE MEATBALLS:

2 to 3 slices of white bread, crusts removed
⅔ cup (160 ml) milk
2 pounds (900 g) ground beef
2 tablespoons (20 g) minced onion
2 tablespoons (8 g) chopped parsley
2 eggs
2 tablespoons (28 ml) olive oil
2 teaspoons salt
1 teaspoon black pepper
½ cup (50 g) grated Parmesan cheese
Pinch of nutmeg
1 teaspoon dried marjoram or oregano
4 cloves of garlic, crushed or pressed

FOR COOKING:

About 1 cup (115 g) fine bread crumbs
2 to 3 tablespoons (28 to 45 ml) olive oil
2 to 3 tablespoons (28 to 45 ml) sunflower oil
Strained tomatoes, or tomato sauce
¼ teaspoon salt
Fresh basil leaves

- Soak the crustless bread in the milk for about 5 minutes. If the bread is thoroughly soaked and there is still a puddle of milk in the bowl, add more bread.

- Break up the soaked bread into smaller pieces. Add the ground beef and all the meatball ingredients together. Using your hands, combine everything, handling it gently, more like tossing a salad than kneading bread, until everything is distributed but not uniform. This handling of the meat helps to keep it light.

- Pour some bread crumbs into a dish. Rinse your hands in cold water to keep the meat from sticking while rolling the meat into compact 1-inch (2.5 cm) balls. Traditional Italian meatballs are very small. Roll each meatball in the bread crumbs to cover it. This makes a nice crust while frying and then becomes very tender while cooking in sauce.

- Heat a wide skillet that will fit all of the meatballs in 1 layer on high heat. Pour in the olive and sunflower oil to generously cover the bottom of the pan. Place the meatballs in the pan in 1 layer. Cook, turning frequently, until browned on all sides.

- Tilt the pan, so the oil collects in one spot. Remove about half of the oil with a spoon. Return the pan to low heat and add the tomato sauce and salt. Simmer for 20 minutes, covered with a lid so the moisture doesn't escape. The oils will separate and float to the top in an obvious layer. This is the sign it is finished. Take off the heat, keep warm, and add the torn basil leaves right before serving.

Note:

Meatballs in tomato sauce are a special-occasion dish in southernmost Italy, specifically in Puglia, Calabria, and Sicily. They are served on their own, with bread perhaps, but never with pasta. Meatballs, being special, are highlighted on their own, with the most simple of tomato sauces. Using strained tomatoes, without seeds or chunks, makes a velvety sweet sauce. These are simple to pull together, make great leftovers, and you can serve them with pasta if you desire.

USA

} # LITTLE ITALY SPAGHETTI AND MEATBALLS

Yield: 15 large meatballs; 5 to 6 servings

FOR THE TOMATO SAUCE:

2 tablespoons (28 ml) olive oil

8 or 9 cloves of garlic, minced

2 large cans (28 ounces, or 785 g each) crushed tomatoes

Red pepper flakes, optional

Pinch of dried oregano

Big pinch of salt

FOR THE MEATBALLS:

2 pounds (900 g) ground beef chuck

1 cup (250 g) ricotta cheese

2 eggs

2 teaspoons salt

½ cup (60 g) bread crumbs

¼ cup (15 g) chopped parsley

1 teaspoon dried oregano

¼ teaspoon red pepper flakes

1½ teaspoons whole fennel seeds

Oil for cooking

FOR SERVING:

Spaghetti

Parmesan cheese

- Choose a wide and deep pan, like a Dutch oven or deep sauté pan, to make the sauce. Heat the olive oil and garlic until it turns golden. Add the tomatoes and seasonings. Bring to a simmer and keep warm to await the meatballs.

- Mix the ground beef, ricotta cheese, eggs, salt, bread crumbs, parsley, oregano, red pepper flakes, and fennel seeds in a bowl. Mix with your hands. Keep things light, like tossing a salad, not like kneading bread. Scoop under the meat with your hand, lifting up, and let it fall through your fingers. Repeat this again and again until everything is well distributed.

- Form large balls, 3 inches (7.5 cm) across or even the size of a baseball. Make them compact, without cracks, but not compressing them too much.

- Heat a skillet with a good glug of olive oil over high heat. When it is very hot, add in as many meatballs as will fit without being crowded. Fry them so they are browned on the outside. Some people like to put them raw into the sauce to cook, but pan-frying them first develops more flavor, makes a nice crust, and helps them hold together better. When browned, but not yet cooked through, remove from the pan and put into the tomato sauce. Repeat with all the meatballs.

- With all the meatballs now in the tomato sauce, let it simmer for around an hour. The longer it simmers, the more deeply flavored everything will be (see Note). The meatballs will finish cooking in the sauce. If it seems the level of sauce is low, or if it gets too thick, it is perfectly okay to add some water; do not fear.

- Bring a big pot of salted water to a rolling boil and add in the spaghetti. Cook according to package directions, usually 9 to 11 minutes for al dente pasta. Drain in a colander and return the pasta to the pot. Straight away, scoop some of the sauce over the spaghetti and stir it to coat. Serve up portions on each dish, with a couple of meatballs, extra sauce, and lots of Parmesan cheese.

Note:

Italian-American meatballs are big, flavorful, and served on top of lots of spaghetti. The story is, for immigrants, meat was more affordable in America than it was in Italy, and they made the meatballs big to celebrate this abundance. Some cooks use a slow cooker to cook the sauce and meatballs. My mother-in-law puts huge, baseball-size meatballs, sauce, and Italian sausages into a slow cooker and lets them cook all day.

} ALBONDIGAS WITH TOMATO SAUCE

Yield: *25 medium meatballs; 4 to 5 servings*

FOR THE MEATBALLS:

½ cup (63 g) masa, ground precooked corn flour
½ cup (120 ml) cold water
½ teaspoon salt
1 teaspoon corn oil
1 pound (455 g) ground beef
1 onion, diced
1 tablespoon (4 g) chopped parsley
1 cup (100 g) grated Parmesan cheese
1 egg
1 teaspoon salt
2 tablespoons (28 ml) olive oil

FOR THE TOMATO SAUCE:

2 medium onions, diced
3 cloves of garlic
Pinch of salt
1½ cups (355 ml) chicken or vegetable stock
2 cups (490 g) tomato sauce
2 tablespoons (5 g) chopped fresh basil
Fresh ground black pepper

FOR SERVING:

Cooked pasta
Parmesan cheese

- Stir the masa, water, salt, and corn oil in a bowl. Knead it together until quite smooth.

- Add the ground meat and all remaining meatball ingredients to the masa dough. Mix it all very well; hands are the best tool for this. Use wet hands to keep the meat from sticking. Form 1½-inch (3.8 cm) balls of the meat mixture. Place on a plate and chill in the fridge for 1 hour.

- To make the sauce, cook the onions, garlic, and a pinch of salt in a large pot with ½ cup (120 ml) of the chicken stock. Simmer this for a few minutes until the onions are tender. Turn the heat to medium low and make sure the onions form a layer on the bottom of the pan and there is still some liquid. Add the meatballs on top of the onions. Cover the pot and cook for 15 minutes. The meatballs will steam atop the onions.

- Add the remaining broth and tomato sauce and simmer uncovered for 10 to 15 minutes more. Add basil and salt and fresh ground pepper to taste.

- Serve the sauce and meatballs over al dente pasta sprinkled with Parmesan cheese.

Tip:
Substitute quick-cooking grits or bread crumbs for the traditional masa corn flour.

GREECE

} **LAMB MEATBALLS**

with Baked Yogurt Sauce

Yield: *18 medium meatballs; 4 to 6 servings*

1 pound (455 g) ground lamb

1½ large red onions, minced

2 cloves of garlic, minced

⅓ cup (20 g) chopped flat-leaf parsley

½ teaspoon dried oregano

¾ teaspoon (plus a little more) salt and black pepper

1½ tablespoons (23 ml) red wine vinegar, divided

1½ cups (345 g) plain cow or goat yogurt

2 eggs

Pinch of salt

- Combine the meat, onions, garlic, herbs, salt, pepper, and ½ tablespoon of the vinegar in a large bowl. Knead and squeeze the meat and onion mixture for a minute or two in order to combine it well. Cover the meat and rest it in the fridge for at least 30 minutes.

- Preheat the oven to 375°F (190°C or gas mark 5). Oil a glass or ceramic baking dish. Roll pieces of the lamb mixture into torpedo shapes by rolling and compressing them in between the fingers and the palm of your hand. Each should be about the width of your palm. Place in the oiled dish. Bake, turning once, about 30 minutes.

- Meanwhile, mix the yogurt with the eggs, 1 tablespoon (15 ml) vinegar, and salt and pour over the meatballs. Shake the dish so the yogurt covers the bottom. Continue to bake until the yogurt sets, 15 to 20 minutes. Remove from the oven and serve hot.

Note:

The yogurt sets into a light custard sauce. It may look a bit curdled in places where the meat juices collect. Don't be concerned; it is delicious!

Red onion

ARGENTINA

GRILLED BEEF MEATBALLS

with Chimichurri Sauce

Yield: *24 large meatballs; 4 to 5 servings*

FOR THE CHIMICHURRI SAUCE:

2 cups (120 g) flat-leaf parsley
1 cup (16 g) fresh cilantro
½ cup (32 g) fresh oregano leaves
4 cloves of garlic
½ teaspoon salt
⅓ cup (80 ml) red wine vinegar
¾ cup (175 ml) extra virgin olive oil

FOT THE MEATBALLS:

1½ pounds (680 g) ground beef (15 % fat)
1½ teaspoons salt
¼ teaspoon black pepper
Skewers (Soak in water, if wooden.)

* Make the chimichurri sauce in a food processor or finely chop all the herbs by hand. In the bowl of the food processor, place the herbs, garlic, salt, and vinegar. Pulse several times until chopped. Slowly pour the oil down the feed tube while the food processor is set ON and blend for about 1 minute until the herbs are chopped very fine. Set aside.

* Place the ground beef in a mixing bowl with salt and pepper. Add 2 tablespoons (28 ml) of the chimichurri sauce to the steak. Mix the meat into the sauce by hand. When combined, form 2½-inch (6.3 cm) balls of meat and thread them onto skewers, about 4 to each stick.

* If cooking on an outdoor grill, oil the grill bars and start the cooking in the hottest area, so the outsides of the meatballs char. Then move the skewers to an area with less heat to continue cooking through. In total, it may take 10 to 15 minutes.

* For cooking on an indoor grill pan, first place a baking tray of kebabs under the oven broiler or in a hot 400°F (200°C, or gas mark 6) oven for about 6 minutes. This gets the cooking started evenly and firms up the kebabs. Now you can transfer them to a hot grill pan or griddle. Allow them to blacken in places before turning them over. Cook about 6 minutes more until the balls are cooked through.

* Serve with lots of chimichurri sauce alongside.

Tip:

Chimichurri improves overnight, so if you can make it a day or two ahead, it will be even better as the flavors meld. Or simply make sure you make enough to have leftovers to enjoy! It will keep in the fridge for a week.

TURKEY

} **MEATBALL KEBABS**

Yield: *40 small meatballs; 8 servings*

FOR THE MEATBALLS:

1 large onion, grated

*2 pounds (900 g) ground lamb,
  or part ground beef*

2 teaspoons salt

2 teaspoons ground cumin

2 teaspoons dried oregano

2 teaspoons dried mint

1 teaspoon Aleppo chile, or sweet paprika

1 teaspoon black pepper

8 or 9 skewers, soaked if wooden

SERVING SUGGESTIONS:

Grilled onions

Tomatoes

Cooked rice

Pita bread

Hummus

- Line a baking tray with foil for holding the skewers before cooking.

- Grate the onions on a box grater or a food processor, which results in less crying from the onion. Combine with the ground lamb, salt, and spices. Mix the meat by hand, squeezing and kneading until it is quite smooth. Roll ½-inch (13 mm) balls and thread them onto the skewers, with each meatball touching the one next to it, 4 or 5 to each stick.

- If cooking on an outdoor grill, oil the grill bars and start the cooking in the hottest area so the outsides char. Then move them to less heat to cook through. In total it may take 10 to 15 minutes.

- To cook on an indoor grill pan, first place the baking tray of kebabs under the oven broiler or in a hot 400°F (200°C, or gas mark 6) oven for about 6 minutes. This gets the cooking started evenly and firms up the kebabs. Now you can transfer them to a hot grill pan or griddle. Allow them to blacken in places before turning over. Cook about 6 minutes more until the balls are cooked through.

- Eat hot or at room temperature with grilled onions, tomatoes, and rice. Or stuff them inside pita breads with onions and hummus.

AUSTRALIA

} **GRILLED BBQ MEATBALLS**

Yield: 40 small meatballs; 8 servings

FOR THE BBQ SAUCE:

1 medium onion, minced

4 fresh plum tomatoes, minced,
    or ½ cup (73 g) plain sauce

⅓ cup (50 g) brown sugar

1 tablespoon (15 ml) Worcestershire sauce

1 to 2 tablespoons (15 to 28 ml) cider vinegar

½ teaspoon smoked paprika

About ¼ teaspoon salt

FOR THE MEATBALLS:

1½ pounds (680 g) lean ground beef or kangaroo

2 eggs

¾ cup (90 g) bread crumbs

2 to 3 rashers of bacon, finely chopped

1 small onion, grated

2 cloves of garlic, minced

3 tablespoons (18 g) chopped green scallion tops

⅓ cup (85 g) BBQ sauce

1 teaspoon salt

Oil cooking spray

Soaked bamboo skewers

FOR SERVING:

Additional BBQ sauce

Fresh salad

- For the BBQ sauce, cook the onion, tomato, and sugar on medium heat, stirring until the sugar dissolves, and then cook about 7 minutes more for the vegetables to soften. Add the remaining ingredients and simmer for 10 minutes so it thickens a bit. Taste and season with more salt or vinegar if necessary.

- Combine the meat and all ingredients for the meatballs in a mixing bowl. Mix well by hand until everything is well distributed. With wet hands to keep the meat from sticking, form small balls, 1½ inches (3.8 cm) across, and line up on a tray. Thread 3 to 5 meatballs on each skewer, depending on length.

- With the grill on medium-high heat, oil the grate to prevent sticking. Cook the meatball skewers for 5 to 7 minutes, turning several times to reach all sides. Serve with lots of BBQ sauce and crispy fresh salad.

Tip:

If outdoor grilling is not a possibility, put the meatballs in a roasting pan, not touching each other, and cook in a preheated 400°F (200°C, or gas mark 6) oven for 10 to 15 minutes. Turn them over once or twice in that time. Smother them in BBQ sauce, returning to the oven for 3 minutes. Kangaroo, like venison and rabbit, is incredibly lean and high in protein. It will cook more quickly than beef.

MIDDLE EAST

} # PISTACHIO LAMB MEATBALLS
with Sweet and Sour Pomegranate Glaze

Yield: 30 small meatballs; 5 servings

FOR THE MEATBALLS:

1 pound (455 g) ground lamb
½ cup (62 g) pistachios, shelled and finely chopped
1 egg
1 teaspoon salt
1 teaspoon ground cumin
¼ cup (30 g) bread crumbs
1 tablespoon (15 ml) water or pomegranate juice

FOR THE GLAZE:

½ cup (170 g) pomegranate molasses (See Tip.)
2 tablespoons (19 g) brown sugar or (20 g) honey
¾ teaspoon salt
¼ teaspoon black pepper
Small pinch of cayenne pepper

FOR THE GARNISH:

Chopped pistachios
Pomegranate seeds

FOR SERVING:

Cooked rice

- Preheat the oven to 450°F (230°C, or gas mark 8). Oil the bottom of a baking dish, about 12 x 14 inches (30 x 36 cm).

- To make the meatballs, combine the lamb with all the other meatball ingredients and mix with wet hands until well combined. With wet hands, roll 1½- to 2-inch (3.8 to 5 cm) balls of the mixture. Place the meatballs into the baking dish so that there is space between them. This allows more surface to brown. Bake for 12 minutes.

- Meanwhile, combine the ingredients for the glaze, whisking it all together. Pomegranate molasses varies in flavor and viscosity, so heat it if necessary to mix everything together and taste the glaze to ensure it is not too sweet or too sour.

- Temporarily remove the meatballs from the oven. Brush or spoon the glaze over each ball, basting them. The glaze will pool in the pan. Return the pan to the oven for 5 minutes.

- Serve them hot with the glaze and pomegranate seeds and chopped pistachios scattered on top. They make a nice appetizer or main dish when alongside rice.

Tip:

Pomegranate molasses can be found in Middle Eastern and Indian markets, or check the international aisle of your grocery store. You can make your own by simmering 3 cups (700 ml) pomegranate juice with ⅓ cup (75 g) brown sugar or (115 g) honey and a squeeze of lemon juice, for about an hour, until it has reduced to about ¾ cup (255 g) in volume and is thick and sticky. Freshly made pomegranate molasses will keep in the fridge for six months and is very good in soda water and cocktails, so make some extra!

}

JEWEL-STUFFED BISON MEATBALLS WITH MUSTARD GLAZE

Yield: *25 small meatballs; 2 to 4 servings*

FOR THE MEATBALLS:

3 shallots, minced

2 tablespoons (28 ml) olive oil

3 dried dates, minced, divided

1 teaspoon caraway seed

1 teaspoon celery seed

½ teaspoon dried savory or crushed rosemary

3 tablespoons (19 g) finely chopped almonds

1 teaspoon salt

¼ teaspoon black pepper

1 pound (455 g) ground bison or lean beef

FOR THE GLAZE:

2 teaspoons Dijon mustard

2 tablespoons (28 ml) pomegranate vinegar

¼ teaspoon anchovy paste

½ tablespoon (10 g) honey

¼ cup (60 ml) white wine

FOR SERVING:

Cooked rice

- In a small skillet on low heat, sauté the shallots, oil, and half of the dates for a few minutes until the shallots are soft. Remove to a mixing bowl.

- Add the caraway seed, celery seed, savory, almonds, salt, and pepper to the shallots. Mix well. Once the shallots are cool, add the ground meat. Mix by hand, squeezing the ingredients together. When the shallots and meat have combined to one mass, form small 1-inch (2.5 cm) meatballs from the mixture. Place them on a foil-lined baking tray.

- Preheat the broiler. Cook the tray of meatballs under the broiler for 3 to 5 minutes to cook through, shaking them often to cook evenly. Remove from the oven.

- Mix the mustard, vinegar, anchovy paste, honey, remaining dates, and wine together. Heat in the microwave for a few seconds if the honey will not dissolve.

- Drain off any collected fat from the tray of meatballs. Pour the mustard sauce over the meatballs, tossing to coat. Return to the broiler for 1 to 2 minutes so the sauce sizzles and sets onto the meatballs.

- Remove and eat while warm. Rice steamed with spices is a nice pairing.

Dates

Caraway seeds

ISRAEL

}

SMOKY, SPICED SUMAC MEATBALLS

Ketzitzot

Yield: *25 medium meatballs; 5 servings*

FOR THE MEATBALLS:

1 teaspoon whole cumin seeds
1½ pounds (680 g) mixed veal and lamb
1 egg
1 cup (60 g) chopped parsley
6 cloves of garlic, minced
1 large onion, grated
3 tablespoons (21 g) bread crumbs
1½ teaspoons salt
2 teaspoons ground sumac
2 tablespoons (28 ml) safflower oil

FOR SERVING:

Fresh parsley
Tahini
Pita bread

- Toast the cumin seeds in a dry pan on high heat, shaking often, until the seeds release their fragrance. Immediately dump them into a mortar and pestle. Pound the seeds a little bit. There's no need to pulverize them; just break them up a bit.

- In a mixing bowl, combine the meats with the egg, parsley, garlic, grated onion, bread crumbs, salt, and sumac. Mix everything together by hand, squeezing and kneading until it is fairly smooth. Form balls or the traditional oval shapes by rolling a bit of meat mixture between your hands and then closing one fist over the ball a few times. Line up on waxed paper or a wet plate to await cooking.

- Heat the oil in a large frying pan over high heat. Transfer the meatballs into the pan. Sear dark brown on all sides, about 4 minutes. Reduce the heat to the lowest setting to finish the cooking, about 5 minutes.

- Serve with a sprinkle of fresh parsley, a drizzle of tahini (page 159), and warm pita bread.

Note:

Sumac powder has an amazing bright sour flavor and magenta color. It is used like lemon or tamarind to give a tangy taste to food. Once you begin to look for it, you may find sumac all around you, in spice shops, Middle Eastern and Armenian grocery stores, and even on the trees around you. There are over 250 types of sumac bushes around the world, growing from tropical to temperate climates. They can be identified by the brilliant red "horns" of berries that grow upward and turn dark red in the fall.

INDIA

} # GREEN KOFTA CURRY

Yield: *10 small meatballs; 2 to 3 servings*

FOR THE MEATBALLS:

½ of an onion
⅓ cup (5 g) cilantro
½ teaspoon cumin seeds
1 to 2 green chilies
4 peppercorns
12 ounces (340 g) mixed ground meat, pork or lamb
¾ teaspoon salt
1 egg yolk

FOR THE ONION SAUCE:

1 tablespoon (14 g) ghee, or butter
1½ medium onions, cut in thin slices and divided
2 cloves of garlic, minced
1 teaspoon ground coriander
1 tablespoon (6 g) fresh ginger, sliced
½ teaspoon turmeric
3 cardamom pods, crushed
2 whole cloves
1 cinnamon stick
1 ripe medium tomato, chopped
1 cup (235 ml) water
Pinch of salt
Small handful of cilantro

FOR SERVING:

Cooked basmati rice

- To make the green meatballs, put half an onion, cilantro, cumin, chilies, and peppercorns into a food processor or blender. Blend until it is a finely chopped paste. Add the green paste into a mixing bowl with the ground meat, salt, and egg yolk. Rinse your hands under cold water to protect them from the chilies and mix the meat by squeezing it until it is smooth and blended. Rinsing hands in cold water again, roll balls into 1-inch (2.5 cm) sized portions. Rinse hands well in cold water before washing with soap and hot water. The oil in chilies which causes a burning sensation on skin must enter through pores or cuts to sting, and rinsing hands under cold water keeps the pores closed and protected.

- In a heavy sauté pan, heat a little bit of the ghee over medium high heat. Once hot and shimmering, add the meatballs. Cook for about 8 minutes until browned in many spots. The meatballs are soft, so be cautious when turning them over not to break them; they firm up once they cook a little bit. Once they are brown, but not yet cooked through, remove them from the pot to a plate.

- There should be about 1 tablespoon (15 ml) of hot oil remaining in the pot; add more ghee if needed. Add the remaining sliced onions, garlic, coriander, ginger, turmeric, cardamom, cinnamon, and cloves. Cook on medium heat, allowing the onions to sizzle, stirring often and scraping the spices off the bottom. After about 5 minutes, the onions will be soft, wilted, and a beautiful yellow color.

- Add the chopped tomato and stir in. If your tomato is very ripe and watery, it will deglaze the bottom of the pan, but if it doesn't, add a splash of water and scrape all the spicy bits off the bottom of the pot. Cook for 1 to 2 minutes. Return the meatballs to the pot on top of the onion. Add the remaining water, salt, and the cilantro. Cook at a simmer for 30 minutes. The sauce is done when the onion sauce has reduced and thickened.

- Serve hot over basmati rice.

SOUTH AFRICA

} # GRILLED APRICOT AND OSTRICH KEBABS

Yield: *16 large meatballs; 4 servings*

FOR THE APRICOT MARINADE:

1 large onion, diced
½ tablespoon butter
½ cup (120 ml) water
3 tablespoons (60 g) apricot jam
½ cup (120 ml) apple cider vinegar
¼ teaspoon dry mustard
1 bay leaf
2 teaspoons brown sugar
Salt and black pepper

FOR THE KEBABS:

2 pounds (900 g) ground ostrich meat
  (or emu/beef/lamb)
½ of a red onion, grated
1½ teaspoons salt
1 teaspoon or more spicy hot sauce
2 tablespoons (28 ml) apricot marinade
2 purple onions, cut in wedges
14 dried apricots, or 7 fresh
Bamboo or metal skewers

- To make the marinade, cook the onion and butter on high heat in a saucepan until softened and toasted brown. Add the water and all other ingredients in the marinade. Bring to a boil, stir to combine, and cook for 3 minutes on high heat. Then remove the marinade from the heat and cool.

- To make the kebabs, put the ostrich meat in a bowl with the onion, salt, hot sauce, and 2 tablespoons (28 ml) of the marinade. Mix by hand so everything is very well combined. Using wet hands so the meat doesn't stick, roll it into compact 2-inch (5 cm) balls.

- Assemble the skewers by alternating wedges of onion with meatballs and apricots. If using fresh apricots, halve them and remove the pit. Brush apricots and onions with a little olive oil so they cook and don't burn. Brush the meatballs with a bit of the marinade.

- With the grill on high heat, oil the grate. Grill the kebabs 4 or 5 minutes on each side. Be careful to avoid overcooking the ostrich as it is very lean and can dry out quickly. Midway through cooking, baste the meatballs with some of the marinade. Repeat once more when ready to remove from the heat.

- These are best eaten in the great outdoors, straight off the sticks.

} APPLE AND FENNEL KOTLECKY

Yield: *14 large meatballs; 4 servings*

½ pound (225 g) ground pork

½ pound (225 g) ground beef

½ of an onion, minced (about ⅔ cup [107 g])

1 teaspoon salt

½ teaspoon black pepper

1 egg

⅓ cup (20 g) chopped parsley

1 cup (150 g) minced apple

1 tablespoon (6 g) whole fennel seeds

1 to 2 tablespoons (15 to 28 ml) safflower oil, for frying

- In a mixing bowl, knead all the ingredients together until they can form a cohesive ball.

- Heat a heavy-bottomed frying pan on high heat with the oil. Form a portion of the meat mixture into a 4-inch-long (10 cm) egg shape and flatten to ¾ inch (2 cm) thick so it becomes an oval patty. Place the patty into the hot oil. Repeat with all the meat mixture, making sure to fry them in batches, not crowding the pan. Cook about 3 minutes on each side for a well-browned crust.

- After the patties brown but are not yet cooked through, remove them to a medium saucepan. Pile them up in the pan. The juices will begin to collect. When all the patties are in the saucepan, pour an ounce (28 ml) of water into the pan, cover with a lid, and put onto high heat. When the water at the bottom of the pan boils, turn the heat to low, keep covered, and cook for 15 minutes. This finishes the cooking by steaming, resulting in a very moist and tender kotlecky.

Fennel

Apple

CHINA

} **SPICY SICHUAN MEATBALLS**

Yield: 15 large meatballs; 3 servings

FOR THE MEATBALLS:

Oil for frying, 1 to 2 cups (235 to 475 ml)
1 pound (455 g) ground lean pork or beef
¼ cup (12 g) minced chives
2 tablespoons (12 g) minced fresh ginger, peeled
5 cloves of garlic, minced
1 egg
¼ cup (48 g) potato starch or (32 g) cornstarch
¼ cup (60 ml) water

FOR THE SAUCE:

¼ cup (64 g) red chile bean paste, doubanjiang
1 to 2 teaspoons Sichuan pepper
2 tablespoons (28 ml) dark soy sauce
2 tablespoons (28 ml) dry sherry
2 tablespoons (26 g) sugar
1 tablespoon (15 ml) Chinkiang black vinegar

FOR SERVING:

Cooked white rice

- Heat the frying oil in a wok. It should be at 350°F (180°C). A piece of chive or bread should sizzle violently on immediate contact with the oil. Avoid getting the oil so hot that it smokes.

- In a large mixing bowl, combine the ground pork, chives, ginger, half of the minced garlic, and egg. Mix it well, kneading and squeezing the meat through your fingers to make it quite smooth. Form 2-inch-wide (5 cm) balls from the mixture and set onto waxed paper; there will be about 15.

- Mix the starch and water in a bowl to make a slurry. Dip several meatballs into the slurry, shake off the excess, and lower them into the oil. Fry until evenly browned, about 5 minutes, turning over a few times while cooking. Work in 3 to 4 batches, as to not crowd the oil. Remove with a slotted spoon to drain on paper towels. Repeat with all the meatballs.

- To make the sauce, remove all the oil except 3 tablespoons (45 ml) of it. Place the wok over high heat. Add the remaining garlic and cook for 30 seconds until just golden. Add the bean paste, Sichuan pepper, soy sauce, sherry, sugar, and vinegar and stir together till smooth. Bring the sauce to a boil and cook for about 4 minutes so it thickens. Add the meatballs into the sauce, tossing to glaze them well. Cook together for another 4 minutes. Test 1 meatball to ensure they are cooked through.

- Serve with plain white rice to counter the spicy sauce.

GERMANY

} **POACHED MEATBALLS IN CAPER CREAM SAUCE**

Konigsberg Klopse

Yield: *16 large meatballs; 4 servings*

FOR THE MEATBALLS:

1 slice of old bread

¼ cup (60 ml) milk

1 pound (455 g) mixed mincemeat, such as beef, pork, veal, or wild boar

1 small onion, finely chopped

4 sardine fillets, or 2 whole sardines, finely chopped (See Tip.)

1 egg

⅓ teaspoon salt

Fresh ground black pepper

About ⅓ cup (42 g) all-purpose flour

FOR COOKING:

4 cups (950 ml) vegetable stock

1 bay leaf

2 whole allspice

1 grate nutmeg

6 peppercorns

FOR THE SAUCE:

½ cup (120 ml) cream

2 egg yolks

1 tablespoon (14 g) butter

Zest from 2 lemons

1 to 2 tablespoons (4 to 8 g) finely chopped parsley

4 tablespoons (36 g) capers

1 small pinch of sugar

- Soak the stale bread in the milk for 10 minutes. Help the bread break down by squeezing it with your fingers until it is pulp. Add the meat, onion, chopped sardines, egg, salt, and pepper to the bread and milk. Mix the ingredients by hand, only until they are combined. The mix will still be irregular. Lumps of bread and pieces of sardine are okay.

- Roll the mixture into portions the size of golf balls. Put the flour on a dish and roll each meatball in it to coat.

- Bring the stock, bay leaf, and spices to a boil. Turn down to a steady, slow simmer. Poach the meatballs in batches; do half of them at a time. First they will sink. When they float they are nearly done; cook 4 minutes more. Remove to a dish and cover to keep warm. Repeat with all the meatballs.

- Bring only the stock to a boil and leave it a while to reduce it by half, looking for a volume of 2 cups (475 ml) to make the cream sauce. Remove the spices from the stock and turn down the heat so the liquid just simmers. Beat the cream and egg yolks together in a glass measuring cup. A few drops at a time, whisk ¼ cup (60 ml) of the hot stock into the cream. Slowly pour the remaining stock into the cream sauce, whisking continuously.

- Return the sauce to the pan, keeping it warm on low heat. Add the butter, lemon zest, parsley, capers, and sugar. Taste the sauce and add salt to taste since all stocks and capers will have different salt content. If you feel there is "something missing" from the sauce, squeeze in just a little lemon juice. Serve the meatballs warm and coated in the sauce.

Note:

Koningsberg Klopse are traditional meatballs from the Prussian city of Koningsberg, a historical center of learning and culture. The city, now an annex of Russia named Kaliningrad, sits near the Baltic Sea. The meatballs highlight the bounty of the northern land and the sea. German and Polish peoples still serve and enjoy these meatballs in memory of Koningsberg.

Tip:

Sardines or anchovies could be used here. They impart a signature flavor. If you use salt-packed anchovies, make sure to rinse them first.

SWEDEN

} SWEDISH MEATBALLS

Yield: 30 medium meatballs; 4 servings

FOR THE MEATBALLS:

¼ cup (60 ml) heavy cream
2 slices of bread, cubed, no crusts
2 cups (320 g) minced red onion
2 teaspoons butter
8 ounces (225 g) ground beef
8 ounces (225 g) ground veal
8 ounces (225 g) ground pork
1 egg
½ teaspoon allspice
½ teaspoon black pepper
1½ teaspoons salt
2 tablespoons (40 g) honey

FOR THE SAUCE:

1 tablespoon (14 g) butter, for frying
2½ tablespoons (20 g) all-purpose flour
1½ cups (355 ml) beef stock
⅓ cup (80 ml) heavy cream
½ teaspoon pickle juice
Salt and pepper, to taste

FOR SERVING:

Egg noodles
Parsley
Sautéed mushrooms (optional)

* Combine the cream and bread in a large mixing bowl. Wait 10 minutes for the bread to soften and absorb all the liquid.

* Sauté the minced red onion with the butter on medium-low heat for about 5 minutes. The onion will be translucent and tender when done.

* Mash up the soaked bread with a fork or your hands. Add the onion to the bowl, along with the ground meat, egg, spices, salt, and honey. Mix with your hands until just combined. With wet hands, roll compact 1½-inch (3.8 cm) balls and line them up on waxed paper to await cooking.

* Heat a heavy skillet on high heat. (See Note.) Melt the tablespoon (14 g) of butter. When hot, add the meatballs. Cook them in batches if the size of the pan cannot accommodate them all. Cooking on high heat, roll the meatballs around occasionally so they brown on all sides. Once browned, turn the heat to low or medium low for about 10 minutes until cooked through. A meat thermometer should read 160°F (71°C) at the center or cut one in half to be sure. When cooked, remove the meatballs from the pan to make the gravy.

* If there is lots of oil in the pan, scoop out all but 1 tablespoon (15 ml). Add the flour, stirring with a wooden spoon. Cook the oil and flour on medium heat, stirring for about 5 minutes. When it is deep nutty brown and smells toasted (don't allow it to burn), pour in the beef stock in a slow steady pour using a whisk to mix it into the roux. Bring the sauce to a low boil, whisking for about 5 minutes. Add the heavy cream, whisking, and the pickle juice. Taste the sauce and add salt and pepper to taste. All boxed, canned, and homemade broths have different amounts of salt, so it is best to use your own judgment. When the sauce is thick and tastes right, add the meatballs. Keep warm until serving.

* Boil the noodles as directed, usually 9 to 11 minutes, and drain. Toss with a little butter or oil and serve on plates with the meatballs and gravy. Garnish with parsley and sautéed mushrooms.

Note:

Frying the meatballs is preferred for taste and tradition. It is also possible to bake them. Place on an oiled pan in a 400°F (200°C, or gas mark 6) oven for 20 minutes. Make the sauce on the stove, add the meatballs into the sauce, and simmer together for 5 to 10 minutes.

POLAND

} **BUCKWHEAT MEATBALLS**

with Mushroom Gravy

Yield: 20 large meatballs; 5 to 6 servings

FOR THE MEATBALLS:

2 onions, minced
4 tablespoons (55 g) butter, divided
2 cups (315 g) cooked buckwheat groats (See Tip.)
12 ounces (340 g) lean ground beef
4 ounces (115 g) ground fatty pork
1 clove of garlic, crushed
2 egg yolks
1 teaspoon salt
¼ teaspoon black pepper
2 egg whites
About ⅓ cup (42 g) all-purpose flour

FOR THE MUSHROOM GRAVY:

8 ounces (225 g) mushrooms, sliced
2 tablespoons (16 g) all-purpose flour
1 cup (235 ml) water or mushroom stock
½ cup (120 ml) heavy cream

FOR SERVING:

Bread
Fresh salad

* In a skillet, sauté the onions in 2 tablespoons (28 g) of butter until tender and golden.

* Put the cooked buckwheat into a bowl. If your groats are whole, bash them up with a wooden spoon so they are smashed but not mashed. This could be done in the food processor also. Add the onions, mixing them up to cool the onions a bit. Add in the ground meats, garlic, egg yolks, salt, and pepper. Knead together until the groats and meat are distributed. If you are grinding your own meat, the old-fashioned way is to grind the cooked buckwheat together with the meat, which results in extra cohesion.

* In a clean bowl, beat the egg whites with a wire whisk. When they fluff to the stage where they hold a peak, add them to the meat. Fold the whipped egg whites into the meat. Whipping the egg whites allows for more lightness in the resulting meatball.

* Put the flour in a dish. Preheat the oven to 350°F (180°C, or gas mark 4).

* Roll the meatballs into balls the size of an egg. Roll each meatball into the flour, shaking to dislodge any excess. Melt the remaining 2 tablespoons (28 g) of butter in a skillet. When hot, brown the meatballs on all sides in the butter. This may need to be done in 2 or 3 batches. As they brown, remove them to a baking dish. Cover the baking dish of meatballs and cook in the preheated oven for 30 to 40 minutes.

* Save the skillet to make gravy. Put the sliced mushrooms into the skillet and cook on medium heat about 6 minutes until the mushrooms are tender. Sprinkle with the flour and cook another minute more. Add the water or stock, scraping up the bits from the bottom. Bring to a boil. Simmer for 10 minutes, add cream, salt, and pepper to taste, and keep warm.

* When the meatballs are removed from the oven, transfer any baking pan drippings into the gravy and stir it in. Serve the meatballs and gravy with bread and fresh salad.

Tip:

Buckwheat groats look like a grain, but they are actually a seed related to rhubarb. Cook according to package directions. The same recipe could also be made with millet or barley. This is great recipe to stretch 1 pound (455 g) of meat to twice the amount.

USA

}

VENISON MEATBALLS

with Wild Berries

Yield: *25 small meatballs; 2 to 4 servings*

FOR THE MEATBALLS:

8 ounces (225 g) mushrooms, minced

1 small onion, minced

2 tablespoons (28 ml) oil or bacon drippings, divided

1 pound (455 g) venison, ground or minced

1 egg

1 teaspoon salt

½ cup (60 g) coarse bread crumbs

All-purpose flour, for dredging

FOR THE SAUCE:

¾ cup (175 ml) beef stock

1 cup (145 g) berries, such as blueberries, cranberries, lingonberries, or huckleberries

½ teaspoon salt

¼ teaspoon black pepper

- In a cast-iron skillet, cook the mushrooms and onions in 1 tablespoon (28 ml) of the oil for about 8 minutes until tender. Remove to a mixing bowl. Add the meat, egg, salt, and bread crumbs, mixing by hand just until combined. Use wet hands to roll into small 2-inch (5 cm) meatballs. Roll each meatball in flour before frying.

- Using the same skillet where the mushrooms were cooked, so as not to lose flavor, heat the remaining tablespoon (15 ml) of oil until shimmering. Add about a third of the meatballs, not crowding the pan. Sear them on all sides and remove to an ovenproof serving dish or baking pan. Repeat with all the meatballs.

- Put the meatball dish in a preheated 250°F (120°C, or gas mark ½) oven for 5 to 8 minutes while making the sauce. This will help them gently cook through. Venison is so lean that it cooks quickly.

- Remove any excess oil from the skillet before adding the beef stock and berries. Bring it to a boil and season well with the salt and pepper, adding more if needed. Boil about 3 minutes to reduce and thicken the sauce a bit. Pour over the meatballs and serve.

Lingonberries

Blueberries

FRANCE

PROVENÇAL RABBIT AND SAGE MEATBALLS

with Roasted Garlic Aioli and Potatoes

Yield: 30 medium meatballs; 5 servings

FOR THE MEATBALLS:

1½ tablespoons (21 g) butter

8 ounces (225 g) mushrooms, minced

1 to 2 shallots, minced

1½ pounds (680 g) ground rabbit

½ pound (225 g) ground pork butt
  (or other fatty pork)

2 to 3 slices of stale white bread, crusts removed,
  ripped into pieces

½ cup (120 ml) wine (Either red or white is okay.)

1 tablespoon (3 g) chopped fresh sage

1 tablespoon (4 g) chopped flat-leaf parsley

2 teaspoons salt

1 egg and 1 egg yolk

FOR THE POTATOES:

2 pounds (900 g) new potatoes, blue, red, yellow,
  or white

4 tablespoons (55 g) of butter

Salt

Black pepper

FOR THE AIOLI SAUCE:

5 or 6 cloves garlic

Yolk of 1 pasturized egg

Pinch of salt

1 cup (235 ml) extra virgin olive oil (Half of this
  can be grapeseed oil for a lighter sauce.)

SERVING OPTIONS:

Fresh bread

Green salad

* For best results, begin this recipe 1 day ahead.

* Melt the butter in a medium-size skillet over medium-high heat. When melted, add the mushrooms and shallots. Stir frequently to sauté. After 5 to 8 minutes, the diced mushrooms will begin to brown and the mushroom liquid will have cooked off. At this point remove it from the heat and cool.

* Combine the rabbit and pork in a bowl together. Mix the 2 meats together by hand, incorporating one with the other. Add the bread, wine, cooled mushroom and shallot mixture, sage, parsley, and salt. Mix it up by hand a little bit so the wine coats everything. Cover well and place in the fridge to marinate overnight. The wine and flavors will marinate the rabbit.

* Prepare the potatoes. Slice them into roughly even sizes, as you prefer. Preheat the oven to 375°F (190°C or gas mark 5).

* Arrange the potatoes on a pan so that they are in 1 layer. Cut the butter into little pieces and toss all over the potatoes. Season with salt and pepper. Place in the hot oven. Remove the pan within the first 5 minutes to toss about the potatoes in the now-melted butter. Make sure all sides are well coated. Cook the potatoes for 1 hour until crispy and golden.

* Place cloves of garlic in a piece of aluminum foil, with a drizzle of olive oil so they won't burn. Close it up to make a packet. Roast in the oven for 40 minutes. When done, the garlic will be soft, silky, spreadable, and sweet. It will also smell amazing. Open the foil packet to cool the garlic.

* While the potatoes and garlic are in the oven, make the meatballs. Remove the marinated rabbit from the fridge, add the egg and 1 egg yolk, and mix the meat by hand. It is okay if there are still lumps of one thing or another. Do try to ensure that the mushy bread is well distributed and the egg is incorporated. With wet hands, roll neat balls nearly the size of the potato pieces. Place these onto a baking tray or roasting pan. Ensure there is 1½ inches (3.8 cm) of space between them so they brown well. Place in the oven and cook for about 15 minutes. Test to ensure they are done before removing from the oven. A thermometer should read 160°F (71°C), and they should be cooked through. Keep warm until serving.

- To make the aioli, squeeze the roasted garlic out of their skins into a mortar and pestle, to be traditional, or a sturdy medium bowl. Add a pinch of salt to the garlic and mash it with a pestle or the back of a spoon. Once the garlic has become a very smooth paste, add the egg yolk, mashing it into the garlic paste. Once it is a homogeneous mixture, switch to a whisk. Whisk in 1 drop of oil. When incorporated, whisk in another. Whisk with purpose, not too fast and not too slow. Repeat adding oil drops in this slow fashion with $\frac{1}{3}$ of the oil. By now an emulsion should be made, meaning you should have a paste that looks like mayonnaise or mustard, not a thin or greasy sauce. Once this emulsion is reached, it is okay to add the olive oil in a slow but steady stream, whisking all the while. It should continue to look like mayonnaise from now on, which is what it is! Once all the oil is added, taste that it has enough salt and adjust as needed.

- If your sauce broke and is thin with little pools of olive oil, then do as follows. Put an egg yolk into a clean bowl, add a drop of the broken aioli, whisk with purpose, and add another drop. Follow the same steps to make the first aioli. You should be all set now. You can make the aioli the day ahead, cover with plastic wrap, and bring to room temperature before serving.

- Serve the potatoes and meatballs together, with aioli in a bowl on the side. Some fresh French bread and a green salad would make a well-balanced meal.

Note:

Rabbit is a commonly eaten meat in France. There are many wonderful traditional dishes of roast rabbit and rabbit stews. It is frequently cooked with wine and mushrooms. As rabbit is a very lean meat, it is often cooked with fatty pork, to tenderize the meat. In these meatballs, we have included all these traditions, so open up a bottle of French wine and imagine yourself having a luncheon on a terrace in Provence, with the breeze smelling like lavender and sage.

SCANDINAVIA

} # ARCTIC CIRCLE ELK MEATBALLS

Yield: *24 small meatballs; 3 to 4 servings*

FOR THE MEATBALLS:

1 small onion, grated
1 teaspoon butter
⅓ cup (38 g) bread crumbs
½ cup (115 g) sour cream
1 egg
½ teaspoon ground allspice
¼ teaspoon ground cloves
1 teaspoon ground black pepper
1 teaspoon salt
1 pound (455 g) ground elk meat
*   (or beef/venison)*

FOR THE GRAVY:

4 tablespoons (55 g) butter
4 tablespoons (31 g) all-purpose flour
3 cups (700 ml) beef stock
Salt and black pepper, to taste

FOR SERVING:

Cooked egg noodles or potatoes
Lingonberry or cranberry sauce

* Cook the onion with the butter in a small pan for about 5 minutes, just to soften it.

* In a large mixing bowl, combine the bread crumbs and sour cream into a thick paste. Stir in the egg, seasonings, and cooked onion, making a uniform mixture. Finally, add in the ground meat and squeeze the meat and sour cream paste together until well distributed and smooth.

* Using wet hands to stop the meat from sticking, roll the meat mixture into small 1-inch (2.5 cm) balls.

* Heat a heavy skillet over high heat with a little bit of butter. Sear the meatballs, rolling them around, just so the outsides brown and turn crispy. It may be necessary to sear the meatballs in batches to avoid crowding the pan. Remove them from the pan before they are cooked through so that the gravy can be made in the same pan.

* Melt the 4 tablespoons (55 g) of butter in the same skillet. Stir the flour into the melted butter, so it is like a paste. It will begin to sizzle, which is fine. Pour in a small splash of the stock and stir it in. Repeat two or three times, adding small amounts of stock at a time and stirring, until the sauce in the pan is thinner with no lumps. Now add the remainder of the stock all at once and scrape up any bits from the bottom. Bring the sauce to a boil and stir so it doesn't stick on the bottom. Turn it down to a simmer, add the meatballs into the gravy, and simmer for 10 more minutes. The gravy will thicken up, and the meatballs will cook through.

* Serve over egg noodles or potatoes with lingonberry or cranberry sauce.

ENGLAND

} # LAMB AND APRICOT MEATBALLS

with Greek Yogurt

Yield: *15 medium meatballs; 4 servings*

FOR THE MEATBALLS:

¼ cup (30 g) chopped walnuts
5 to 6 dried apricots, diced
1 pound (455 g) ground lamb
1 teaspoon salt
⅛ teaspoon allspice
2 cloves of garlic, minced
3 tablespoons (12 g) chopped parsley

FOR SERVING:

Plain Greek yogurt

- Preheat the oven to 375°F (190°C or gas mark 5).

- Mix all the ingredients together in a large bowl, just until everything is well distributed. With wet hands, form 2-inch (5 cm) balls and place them in a greased baking pan.

- Bake for 20 to 25 minutes. Test that the meatballs are done. A meat thermometer should read 160°F (71°C) or cut one in half.

- Serve the yogurt as a sauce alongside the hot meatballs.

Tip:

These meatballs have a compelling sweet and meaty flavor. The yogurt provides balance; stir fresh herbs or spices into it if you wish.

Apricots

Garlic

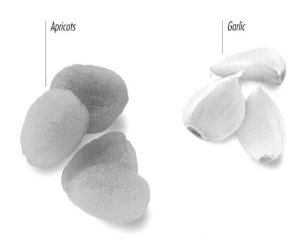

} RICH MEATBALLS AND GRAVY

Yield: *40 small meatballs; 6 servings*

FOR THE MEATBALLS:

2 slices of dry bread
⅓ cup (80 ml) milk
1 pound (455 g) 95% lean ground beef
¼ pound (115 g) sausage meat or ground pork
1 medium onion, grated
2 tablespoons (8 g) chopped parsley
2 egg yolks
1 teaspoon salt
Black pepper

FOR THE SAUCE:

4 tablespoons (55 g) butter
½ cup (63 g) all-purpose flour
2½ cups (570 ml) beef stock
Bouquet garni herbs (1 bay leaf, 1 sprig of parsley,
*   1 sprig or big pinch of thyme, and 1 sprig or*
*   big pinch of sage)*
Salt
Black pepper

SERVING SUGGESTIONS:

Mashed potatoes
Green peas

* Soak the bread and milk in a bowl for about 10 minutes. Break up the bread with your fingers until it is all in small pieces.

* Combine the meats, onion, and parsley. Add the soaked bread, egg yolks, salt, and pepper and mix. Form into small 1-inch balls (2.5 cm), rolling them with wet hands to keep the meat from sticking. Place them on a plate or waxed paper and chill them in the fridge for 30 minutes while beginning the sauce.

* In a heavy sauté pan or Dutch oven, melt the butter over medium-high heat. Mix the flour into the butter with a wooden spoon. Make a roux with the butter and flour by allowing it to boil and fry for about 5 to 10 minutes. You must continue to stir with the wooden spoon the entire time, scraping the entire bottom of the pan and all the edges. The roux will darken shades of brown; take care it does not burn to black. When it becomes a rich brown color, a dark caramel, turn off the heat and stir the beef stock directly in.

* Stir or whisk the sauce until there are no lumps in the roux. Turn the heat on high and bring the sauce to a boil. Add the herbs of the bouquet garni. Keep the sauce at a low boil for 20 minutes. Place the meatballs in the sauce, keep at a simmer, and cook for 15 minutes. Stir occasionally to ensure it is not sticking or burning on the bottom. If your sauce thickens up too much, stir in water until it is a desirable consistency. Season with salt and pepper.

* Serve hot. These meatballs are a wonderful match for mashed potatoes and green peas.

Dry bread | Bouquet garni herbs

ENGLAND

} **NOSE TO TAIL OFFAL MEATBALLS**

Yield: *15 large meatballs; 5 servings*

FOR THE MEATBALLS:

⅓ pound (152 g) caul fat, or 15 strips thin bacon
1½ pounds (680 g) ground lean pork
½ pound (225 g) pork liver
1 pound (455 g) kidney or heart (pork or veal)
1 large onion, grated
¾ cup (90 g) fine bread crumbs
1 teaspoon dried thyme
1 teaspoon dried sage
1 tablespoon (4 g) chopped parsley
Pinch of ground nutmeg
2 teaspoons salt
½ teaspoon black pepper

SERVING SUGGESTIONS:

Mashed potatoes
Green peas

* Soak the caul fat in a bowl of cold water for 20 minutes. Set aside.

* Clean the liver, kidney, or heart very well. Chop them fine, either with a knife or in the food processor. The pieces should be small, but not a purée.

* Mix the meats, onion, bread crumbs, herbs, and spices until combined.

* Preheat the oven to 375°F (190°C, or gas mark 5). Each meatball will be made from ¼ cup (55 g) of the meat mixture and covered with caul fat or bacon. An efficient way to do this is to unroll some of the caul fat onto a cutting board. Place the ball of meat onto it, take a paring knife, and slice off just the part you need to wrap around the ball. Place each fat-wrapped ball onto a heavy baking tray.

* Bake in the oven for 35 to 40 minutes; bacon will take longer to cook than the caul fat. Serve while hot and crispy. They taste right eaten with a strong ale, mashed potatoes, and green peas.

Note:

These traditional British meatballs are wrapped in caul fat, which is a thin web of fat that surrounds various organs. It is sold rolled up and needs to be soaked and unrolled as you use it. It is quite simple and bastes whatever it is draped over in a beautiful fat, making it all luscious and crispy. Thin bacon is an alright replacement.

2

Poultry Balls

◇◇

Poultry is easy to farm, requiring little space and little feed if the birds are left to forage, making them a popular domesticated farm animal in every culture. The meat is mild, relatively lean, and easy to cook. Chicken, turkey, duck, and goose are popular all over the globe. It is estimated that 30 % of all meat consumed is poultry, making it the second most popular meat.

Poultry is a great source of protein, with about one-fifth of the meat absorbed as protein. When purchasing birds or ground meat, they should have no smell. Buy the best meat you can. A real farm-raised, organic bird who spent its life eating a varied diet has an amazing flavor and nutrition profile, which a factory-raised bird injected with antibiotics and fed GMO corn does not. So choose the best bird you can for your health and the flavor.

UKRAINE

} MAMA'S CHICKEN MEATBALL SOUP

Yield: *50 tiny meatballs; 6 to 8 servings*

1 medium white onion
1 carrot
1 to 2 slices of old bread, crusts cut off
⅓ cup (80 ml) milk
1 tablespoon (14 g) butter
8 cups (1.9 L) water
½ teaspoon salt
¼ teaspoon black pepper
1 bay leaf
2 potatoes, diced
1 pound (455 g) ground chicken or turkey
1 egg
1 teaspoon salt
¼ cup (49 g) medium-grain white rice

- Shred first the onion and then the carrot on a box grater, keeping them in separate piles. This can be done in a food processor with the grater attachment. Set aside 3 tablespoons (30 g) of the grated onion to put into the meatballs. You should have nearly equal amounts of carrot and onion.

- Break the bread into pieces and mix it with the milk in a mixing bowl. Let soak for 10 minutes.

- In a soup pot, cook the onion with the butter for about 5 minutes. Add the carrots and cook for 3 or 4 more minutes; the onion and carrot should be soft and glossy. Add the water, salt, pepper, bay leaf, and diced potatoes. Bring the pot of soup to a boil.

- While waiting for the soup to boil, make the meatballs. Mash up the soaked bread with a fork. To the same bowl, add the ground chicken, egg, and salt. Mix up well, using a fork; the mixture will be very loose.

- Add the rice to the soup when it finally comes to a boil and turn it down to a steady simmer. To form little balls of the chicken mixture, first wet your hands with cold water. Pull out a small amount of the meat and place it on the palm of your hand. Curve the fingers on your other hand and use the outside of the little finger, drawing it across the palm, lifting up and rolling the chicken into a more round shape. Repeat this motion 2 or 3 times per ball. Toss them directly into the soup; they will not hold their shape otherwise. If forming them feels like a mess, use 2 little spoons. The meatballs should be the size of hazlenuts.

- Once all the balls are in the soup, continue to simmer for half an hour. Serve steaming hot in soup bowls.

MEXICO

} **RED POZOLE**

with Chicken Meatballs

Yield: *30 small meatballs; 6 to 8 servings*

FOR THE MEATBALLS:

2 slices of stale bread, no crusts
1 pound (455 g) ground chicken or turkey
1 teaspoon garlic powder
1 teaspoon dried oregano, preferably Mexican
1 teaspoon salt

FOR THE POZOLE:

*5 dried New Mexico chiles, no seeds/stems
  (See Tip.)*
3 tablespoons (45 ml) sunflower oil, or canola oil
2 yellow onions
1 whole head of garlic, cloves peeled
4 cups (950 ml) chicken broth
2 cups (475 ml) water, or more
*4 cups (660 g) hominy corn, or 2 cans (14.5
  ounces, or 400 g each) (See Tip.)*

FOR THE SOUP TOPPINGS:

Lime wedges
Sliced radish
Shredded cabbage

- Break the stems off the dried chiles and dump out as many seeds as possible. Place the chiles in a bowl, cover with warm water, and use a plate or a cup to keep them submerged. Soak for 30 minutes to rehydrate. Use caution when handling the chiles and wash your hands with soap and cold water after touching them.

- Soak the crustless bread in tap water. Place in a second mixing bowl and allow it to break down. To the same bowl, add the ground chicken, garlic powder, oregano, and salt. Knead well until nearly uniform.

- Form 1-inch (2.5 cm) balls of the chicken mixture. Heat the oil in a soup pot. Sauté the chicken balls on high heat, in batches if necessary, until golden brown on most sides, about 5 minutes; they will not yet be cooked through. Remove to a plate.

- Add the onion and garlic to the oil. Stir frequently, scraping the bottom, for about 2 minutes. When the onion releases its juices, add the chicken broth and water and scrape any garlic and onion off the bottom. Stir in the hominy. Bring the soup just to a boil before lowering it to a simmer.

- While waiting for the soup to boil, purée the chile skins and the soaking water in a blender or food processor. Purée thoroughly. Strain the thick red liquid through a sieve into the soup. Straining is essential; this removes all the tough bits of chile and any overlooked seeds. All the chile flavor is extracted into the liquid, but not too much of the heat.

- Add all the meatballs into the simmering soup. Add more water to cover if necessary. Simmer 1 hour for best flavor. While the soup simmers, slice the lime, radish, and cabbage. When serving the soup, allow everyone to add their own toppings.

Note:

Don't be put off by the large amount of dried chiles in this soup. The sweet flavor of the chile is in the soup, not the heat. This soup is perfect to serve to a crowd or party. It is even better the next day.

Tip:

Hominy is corn treated by a traditional process called nixtamalization, which makes more nutrients and proteins available and turns the corn into puffy kernels.

BRAZIL

} # XIM XIM NUTTY CHICKEN MEATBALL AND SHRIMP STEW

Yield: *28 small meatballs; 4 servings*

FOR THE STEW:

¼ cup (35 g) unsalted peanuts

¼ cup (35 g) cashews

1 medium onion, quartered

1 clove of garlic

½ of a serrano chile

Handful of cilantro

1 peeled piece fresh ginger (1 inch x 1 inch [2.5 x 2.5 cm])

2 cups (488 g) peeled uncooked shrimp, divided

1½ cups (355 ml) water, divided

¼ cup (60 ml) dendê oil (red palm oil)

1 lime

FOR THE MEATBALLS:

1 pound (455 g) ground or minced chicken

2 teaspoons canola or dende oil

1 teaspoon salt

¼ teaspoon black pepper

1 egg

¾ cup (90 g) bread crumbs

FOR SERVING:

Cooked rice

- Toast the peanuts and cashews in a dry pan on high heat to intensify the flavors. Shake frequently. When some spots are toasted a dark brown, remove from the heat and put into a food processor. Pulse until ground into a fine meal, stopping before it becomes a sticky purée. Add the onion, garlic, chile, cilantro, ginger, half of the shrimp, and half the water. Turn the processor on for about 20 seconds, aiming for a well-pureed, very green paste. Set aside.

- Combine the ingredients for the meatballs. Heat a stew pot on high heat with a little canola oil or dendê oil. With wet hands, roll the chicken mixture into 1-inch (2.5 cm) balls, small enough to eat in one bite. Cook the chicken balls in the oil, rolling around to cook the outsides of all of them.

- When the chicken balls have cooked on the outside, add the green puréed paste of nuts and herbs. Stir it to coat the meatballs; it will sizzle. Add the remainder of the water and the shrimp. Bring it all to a boil and then turn it down to a simmer. Simmer for 30 minutes.

- Take the stew off the heat, taste it, and squeeze in juice from half the lime. Taste it again and add more lime if you like. The stew should be thick; add more water if you like. Serve hot with rice.

Note:

In making this dish, savor the colors and the smells and be transported to another land. The history of the xim xim stew comes to Brazil from the years of the slave trade. West African people were replicating the staple stews of their homelands.

Tip:

Dendê oil is available at Brazilian and African markets, specialty grocery stores, and health food markets. It is made from the fruit of the palm oil tree. In its red and unrefined state it is among the healthiest oils on the globe. It gives a celebratory orange-red hue to everything it touches. Look for sustainably harvested red palm oil. Much palm oil is grown in rainforest regions. Deforestation and destruction of orangutan habitats are a concern, so buy from sustainably run businesses.

} YELLOW GUNDI CHICKEN MEATBALL SOUP

Yield: *20 large meatballs; 6 to 8 servings*

FOR THE SOUP:

⅓ of a medium onion, grated

2 cloves of garlic, crushed

1 stalk of celery, small dice

1 tablespoon (15 ml) olive oil

4 cups (950 ml) good-quality chicken stock

4 to 6 cups (950 ml to 1.4 L) water

1½ pounds (680 g) potatoes, large diced

1 teaspoon turmeric

Salt and ground black pepper, to taste

1 tablespoon (15 ml) lemon juice

Chopped parsley, for serving

FOR THE DUMPLINGS:

1 pound (455 g) ground chicken or turkey

2 medium onions, grated

3 tablespoons (45 ml) vegetable oil

6 ounces (170 g) chickpea flour

1 teaspoon turmeric

½ teaspoon ground cumin

½ teaspoon ground cardamom

½ teaspoon ground coriander

1½ teaspoons salt

4 to 5 tablespoons (60 to 75 ml) cold water

* In a large soup pot over high heat, cook the onion, garlic, and celery with the olive oil. Once the vegetables begin to soften and start to brown, add the chicken stock and water. Add the diced potatoes and turmeric. Bring the soup to a boil. Turn it down to an active simmer. Add a large pinch of salt to taste.

* While the soup is cooking, make the chicken dumplings. Mix everything except the water in a mixing bowl. Add water a spoon at a time, mixing in between. Look for a dough that is smooth. The dumpling dough will be a little sticky. If you make it ahead and allow it to chill for a few hours in the fridge, they will not be sticky to roll. However, they are fine to cook straight away. Simply use 2 soup spoons to make compact balls and drop each one into the simmering soup as it is formed.

* Cook the dumpling soup at a low simmer for 1 hour. Before serving, add the lemon juice and fresh herbs and check that there is enough salt and pepper.

Note:

Gundi is the much-loved Persian chicken soup. The chickpea flour turns meatballs into luscious dumplings.

THAILAND

} **RED CURRY**

with Eggplant, Greens, and Meatballs

Yield: *16 large meatballs; 3 to 4 servings*

FOR THE MEATBALLS:

1 pound (455 g) chicken, ground or minced

1 egg

½ cup (25 g) panko bread crumbs

1 teaspoon salt

Zest from 2 limes

FOR THE CURRY:

2 tablespoons (28 ml) coconut oil or vegetable oil

*4 Asian eggplants, sliced into ½-inch
    (1.3 cm) pieces*

3 tablespoons (45 g) red curry paste

1 can (13 ounces, or 385 ml) coconut milk

4 cups (950 ml) water

4 to 6 scallions, roughly chopped

2 kefir lime leaves

1 tablespoon (15 ml) Thai fish sauce

*4 medium bok choy, halved (or 4 big handfuls of
    cabbage or leafy greens)*

1 handful of Thai basil or sweet basil leaves

Juice of half a lime

SERVING SUGGESTIONS:

Lime wedges

Fresh basil

Cooked noodles or rice

- Combine the meatball ingredients well. Let sit for 10 minutes to stiffen up. Roll 2-inch (5 cm) balls of the mixture.

- Heat a wok over high heat. Once is it blistering hot, add the oil in a stream around the pan and toss in 3 or 4 meatballs, frying them on all sides. Stir them carefully, as to not break them. Use the oil in the wok bottom to baste them and keep them from sticking. When brown, after a minute or two, remove to a plate. Repeat with all meatballs.

- Throw in the eggplant slices. Stir-fry the eggplant, tossing it about for about 3 minutes, until it begins to soften and take on some color. Remove the eggplant and set aside with the meatballs.

- Add the red curry paste to the wok; it will sizzle. Follow right away with ¼ of the coconut milk. Cook 1 minute to really infuse the flavors. Add some of the water, stirring the curry paste into the liquid well, and then add the remaining water, coconut milk, eggplant, meatballs, scallions, lime leaves, and fish sauce. Cook the sauce on a steady simmer for 10 minutes. Add the bok choy, simmering until the greens are tender, about 4 minutes.

- Right before serving, stir in the basil, a squeeze of lime juice, and check if the curry needs some salt. This Thai curry is a great one-pot dish but could be stretched with noodles or white or brown rice. Serve with lime wedges and extra basil.

} JAPANESE YAKITORI CHICKEN MEATBALLS

Yield: *32 small meatballs; 6 servings*

FOR THE YAKITORI SAUCE:

¼ cup (60 ml) cooking sake
¼ cup (60 ml) mirin
¼ cup (60 ml) soy sauce
¼ cup (48 g) palm sugar or raw sugar

FOR THE MEATBALLS:

1⅓ pounds (605 g) ground chicken or turkey
1 teaspoon salt
¼ cup (25 g) chopped scallion
Zest of 1 lemon
3 teaspoons (24 g) fresh grated ginger
8 or 9 wooden skewers, soaked in water
Sesame seeds, for garnish

- Whisk the sake, mirin, soy sauce, and sugar together in a small saucepan. Boil the sauce, reducing until it is about half the original volume.

- The fresh ginger and lemon zest are best grated using a microplane. Knead together the ground chicken, salt, scallion, lemon zest, and ginger.

- Preheat the oven to 375°F (190°C, or gas mark 5) and line a baking tray with aluminum foil. Form 1-inch (2.5 cm) balls of the chicken mixture. Place on the baking tray. Bake the chicken meatballs for 6 minutes. Remove from the oven; they will not yet be cooked through.

- Thread 4 to 5 meatballs onto each skewer. Using an outdoor grill or indoor grill pan, grill on high heat for 1 to 2 minutes. Turn occasionally to allow the chicken meatballs to blacken in parts. Lower the heat and, using a brush, baste the chicken skewers with the yakitori sauce. Cook until the sauce has set. Turn, baste again, and cook. Repeat until the skewers are well glazed.

- Remove from the heat and serve with the remaining sauce. Garnish with sesame seeds and scallion.

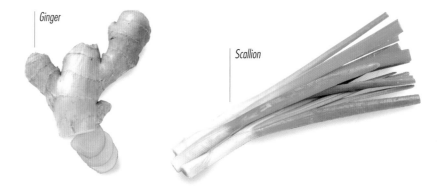

Ginger

Scallion

}

CHICKEN MEATBALLS

with Olives, Feta, and Sun-Dried Tomatoes

Yield: *20 medium meatballs; 4 servings*

Sun-dried tomatoes in oil, 4 halves, blotted dry
3 cloves of garlic, divided
¼ cup (43 g) pitted kalamata olives
¼ cup (30 g) dry plain bread crumbs
¼ cup (38 g) crumbled feta cheese
1 pound (455 g) ground chicken (or turkey)
¼ teaspoon red pepper flakes
1 teaspoon salt
½ teaspoon ground black pepper
1 egg
1 tablespoon (15 ml) milk
¼ cup (31 g) all-purpose flour for dusting
2 tablespoons (28 ml) olive oil
1 can (14½ ounces, or 410 g]) diced canned tomatoes
½ teaspoon dried oregano

* Finely chop, or pulse in a food processor, the sun-dried tomatoes, 2 of the garlic cloves, and the olives. Add the bread crumbs and feta cheese. Pulse or chop it all into a chunky paste.

* Combine the olive and feta paste with the ground chicken, red pepper flakes, salt, pepper, egg, and milk. Mix together with your hands. Roll into small 1½-inch (3.8 cm) balls. Wet your hands with water to help avoid stickiness. Roll each ball in flour.

* Heat the olive oil in a skillet over medium-high heat. When hot, add the meatballs and cook, turning until golden all over, 5 to 6 minutes. Remove from the heat to a plate; the meatballs are not cooked through at this point.

* Mince the remaining clove of garlic. Add the minced garlic, diced tomatoes, and oregano to the skillet where the meatballs were browned. Stir to scrape up the browned bits from the bottom the pan. Return the meatballs to the pan, keeping the sauce at a low simmer. Turn them occasionally and continue cooking until just cooked through, about 3 minutes longer. Cut one in half to test for doneness; simmer longer if necessary.

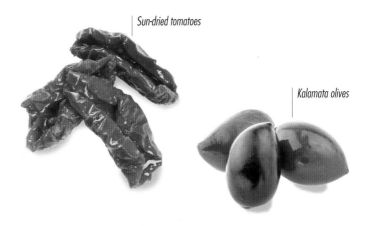

Sun-dried tomatoes

Kalamata olives

MEXICO

} **TACO CHICKEN MEATBALLS**

with Red Salsa Rice

Yield: *16 medium meatballs; 4 servings*

FOR THE RED RICE:

1½ teaspoons canola oil

1½ cups (278 g) long-grain white rice

1 cup (260 g) salsa (canned or fresh)

1 cup (235 ml) water or chicken broth

½ teaspoon salt

FOR THE MEATBALLS:

1 to 2 slices of white bread, crusts cut off

¼ cup (60 ml) milk

1 large onion, diced

1 tablespoon (15 ml) canola oil

1 pound (455 g) ground chicken (or turkey)

1¼ teaspoons salt

1 egg

1 tablespoon (4 g) chopped parsley

2 tablespoons (2 g) chopped cilantro

1 teaspoon garlic powder

¾ teaspoon onion powder

¼ teaspoon black pepper

¾ teaspoon chili powder

¼ teaspoon paprika

1 teaspoon dried oregano

1 teaspoon ground cumin

FOR SERVING:

Lime wedges

Crema or sour cream

• To make the rice, preheat the oven to 350°F (180°C, or gas mark 4). Add the oil and rice to a 3-quart (2.8 L) ovenproof saucepan. Cook over medium heat, stirring frequently, until the grains of rice become milky white. This takes about 5 minutes. Some toasted grains are okay. Add the salsa, water, and salt. Stir well. Allow the pot to come to a full boil.

• Cover the pot of rice, take it off the heat, and place it in the preheated oven. Bake for 25 minutes. Remove from the oven, keep the cover on, and let rest 5 minutes before fluffing the rice with a fork and serving.

• To make the meatballs, soak the bread and milk for 10 minutes in a mixing bowl. It is ready when the bread has soaked up all the milk and turned to mush; add a little more bread if there is still a pool of milk. Sauté the diced onion in oil till tender.

• Prepare a baking tray to hold all the meatballs. Line it with aluminum foil for easy cleanup and spray it with oil. Add everything into the bowl with the milk-soaked bread: the onion, ground poultry, salt, egg, herbs, and spices. Mix everything together with your hands. Form 2-inch (5 cm) balls of the meat mixture and place on the oiled pan. Bake in the 350°F (180°C, or gas mark 4) oven for 20 minutes. When done, a meat thermometer should read 170°F (77°C), and if you cut one open, it should be cooked through with no pink.

• Serve the meatballs and red rice with lime and crema or sour cream.

Tip:

It is easy to add more vegetables into the rice. Defrost 1 cup (130 g) frozen peas, for example, and sneak them into the rice during the last 5 minutes of cooking in the oven.

MOROCCO

} **CHERMOULA CHICKEN BOULETTES**

Yield: 16 medium meatballs; 4 to 5 servings

FOR THE CHERMOULA SAUCE:

4 cloves of garlic

½ cup (8 g) cilantro or parsley (30 g)

Zest of 1 lemon

2 teaspoons paprika

1 teaspoon chili powder

¾ teaspoon ground cumin

½ cup (120 ml) olive oil

FOR THE CHICKEN:

1 pound (455 g) chicken, ground or minced small

1 teaspoon salt

4 to 5 skewers, soaked if wooden

* Place all the ingredients for the chermoula sauce into a blender, which really does a better job than a food processor here. Use whichever one you have. If you don't have either, use a mortar and pestle, adding the oil in small amounts along the way, as everything gets bashed up. Once the sauce is well blended, give it a taste. The spice flavors will blossom when cooked, and the sauce is not an emulsion, so the herbs will settle and it might look chunky; no worries.

* Soak the skewers if wooden. Mix the chicken with the salt. Using wet hands, form compact 1½-inch (3.8 cm) balls of the chicken and thread them onto the skewers. Place them to rest on a foil-lined baking tray. Spoon a little bit of the chermoula onto the uncooked meatballs; they will get more soon.

* Use an outdoor grill or the oven broiler to cook them.

* Under a broiler, line up the skewered chicken, keeping a close eye on it, turning as it browns, for 10 to 12 minutes. Baste several times midway with more chermoula sauce or scoop up the sauce that will accumulate on the pan. They cook very well this way.

* If grilling, brush the grill bars with oil, place the meatball skewers on, and wait several minutes, about 3, for the meatballs to release easily from the grill bars. When they do, turn and cook again on another side. Cook about a total of 10 to 12 minutes; it will vary widely, depending on the size of meatball and heat of the grill.

* In all cooking methods, use a meat thermometer to ensure the chicken is cooked through to 170°F (77°C). When cooked, remove to a platter and drizzle with more of the chermoula sauce.

Note:

These chicken meatballs are very simple, without egg or bread filler. They highlight the spices in the chermoula and perhaps evoke primal cooking over an outdoor fire. Use the best-quality chicken you can and find the beauty in the simplicity.

USA

} # DUCK, PROSCIUTTO, AND PRUNE
Stuffed Meatballs

Yield *14 large meatballs; 4 servings*

8 prunes, cut in quarters
⅓ cup (80 ml) port wine
1 pound (455 g) ground duck
1 teaspoon salt
¼ teaspoon black pepper
½ teaspoon paprika
½ teaspoon allspice
⅓ cup (38 g) coarse bread crumbs
1 egg
2 or 3 slices of prosciutto

* Put the prunes and the port wine into a small saucepan. Warm on low heat for 10 minutes, looking for the prunes to plump up. Remove the prunes to a plate and set both aside to cool.

* Mix the ground duck with the salt, pepper, paprika, allspice, bread crumbs, and egg. Add the cooled port. Mix the meat by hand, squeezing it through your fingers, just until everything is well combined. Let it rest in the fridge for 10 minutes for the bread crumbs to fully soak up the port.

* Meanwhile, cut the prosciutto into 1-inch (2.5 cm) strips, the short way. Take up 2 pieces of the quartered prunes and wrap them in a piece of prosciutto. Place them on a plate and continue with the rest, so you have about 15 prosciutto-wrapped prunes.

* Using wet hands to avoid sticking, take a bit of the duck mixture and flatten it in the palm of one hand. Place one prosciutto-prune packet in the center of the meat. Close your hand and the meat around it to wrap the ground duck snugly around the fruit. Add more ground duck to patch any holes. Roll it into a neat ball that should be about the size of a golf ball. Line up your creations on a well-oiled or parchment paper–lined baking tray.

* Bake in a 400°F (200°C, or gas mark 6) preheated oven for 10 minutes. Turn the meatballs over and bake another 10 minutes. Serve while warm.

USA

}

THANKSGIVING STUFFING TURKEY MEATBALLS

with Cranberry Sauce

◇◇

Yield: *30 large meatballs; 4 to 6 servings*

FOR THE MEATBALLS:

2½ cups (500 g) stuffing (recipe follows)
1 pound (455 g) ground turkey
1 egg
2 tablespoons (8 g) chopped parsley
1 teaspoon salt
Generous fresh ground black pepper

FOR THE STUFFING:

2 tablespoons (28 g) butter
¼ cup (40 g) chopped onion
¼ cup (25 g) chopped celery
Pinch of salt
1 cup (235 ml) chicken stock
2 cups (114 g) seasoned packaged stuffing mix

FOR THE CRANBERRY SAUCE:

1 orange
1 large apple, peel on, large dice
Water
2 cups (200 g) cranberries
1 cinnamon stick
⅛ teaspoon ground cloves
⅓ teaspoon salt
⅓ cup (67 g) sugar, more to taste

* First make the stuffing. Melt the butter in a saucepan and sauté the onion and celery with a pinch of salt, for about 5 minutes, until they are very tender. Add the chicken stock and bring to a boil. Remove from the heat and toss in the seasoned stuffing mix. Cover with a lid or foil for 5 minutes.

* While waiting for the stuffing to soak, begin the cranberry sauce. Peel the zest from the orange in long strips with a vegetable peeler. Peel the orange, roughly dice the fruit, and discard the peel and seeds. Place the orange zest and apples in the saucepan with a little bit of water on low heat to soften them. Once softened, but not yet mush, add the diced oranges, cranberries, cinnamon stick, cloves, and salt. Add water to fill ⅔ of the way up the berries. Bring to a boil, stirring occasionally. When the berries have popped, stir in half the sugar and taste. Add the remaining sugar if needed. Fruits vary in sweetness, so adding sugar and tasting is the best way to judge how much additional sugar is needed. The longer the sauce cooks on the heat, the less chunky it will be. Alter the cooking time for your personal taste and remove from the heat when it is perfect.

* Preheat the oven to 350°F (180°C, or gas mark 4). Line a baking dish with aluminum foil and grease lightly. This step makes cleanup superfast.

* Mix the stuffing with the ground turkey, egg, parsley, and seasonings. Using your hands, roll the mixture into neat 2-inch (5 cm) balls. Place in the prepared baking dish. Bake in the preheated oven for 20 minutes. Midway through baking, shake the pan to roll around the meatballs and help browning on all sides. If they stick to the bottom, return in a few minutes and try again.

* After 20 minutes of baking, the meatballs should be browned and firm. A thermometer at the center of the meatball should read 170°F (77°C) to ensure they are cooked through. Remove the dish from the oven and serve with the cranberry sauce.

AUSTRALIA

} **ORANGE DUCK MEATBALLS**

with Celery Root Purée

Yield: *14 large meatballs; 4 servings*

FOR THE MEATBALLS:

3 cloves of garlic, minced
1 small shallot, minced
1 tablespoon (28 ml) olive oil
1 pound (455 g) ground duck
¾ teaspoon five-spice powder
1 teaspoon salt
2 egg yolks
¼ cup (13 g) panko bread crumbs
1 tablespoon (20 g) honey
Zest from 1 orange
¼ cup (60 ml) juice from the orange

FOR THE CELERY ROOT PURÉE:

1 pound (455 g) celery root (about 2 roots)
1 cup (235 ml) vegetable stock
2 cloves of garlic
½ teaspoon salt
1 tablespoon (14 g) butter
¼ teaspoon white pepper
¼ cup (60 ml) heavy cream

- Quickly sauté the garlic and shallot in the oil just till they turn soft and transparent. Remove them to a mixing bowl. Add the duck and the rest of the meatball ingredients. Combine them all by hand until just incorporated and well distributed.

- Slice the rough outside off the celery root with a knife and discard. Cut the root into small dice and put it in a small saucepan. Pour the vegetable stock into the pan and add the garlic and salt. Cover the pot, bring it to a boil, and turn it down to simmer for 10 to 15 minutes. When the celery root is very tender, take it off the heat. Add the butter, white pepper, and cream. Put all of it into a food processor, in batches if necessary, and purée it until luscious and smooth. If you like, add more cream for a richer dish.

- Roll 2-inch (5 cm) balls of the meat mixture, using wet hands so it does not stick. Place them on a parchment paper–lined baking tray. Bake in a 400°F (200°C, or gas mark 6) preheated oven for 10 minutes. Turn the meatballs over and bake another 5 minutes or until cooked through.

- Serve the meatballs atop a mound of the celery root purée.

INDIA

} **DUCK CURRY MEATBALLS**

with Spicy Onion Chutney

Yield: 30 small meatballs; 6 servings

FOR THE SPICY ONION CHUTNEY:

1 large onion, minced
1½ tablespoons (24 g) tomato paste
1 teaspoon chili powder
1 teaspoon cumin seeds, toasted in a pan
Dash of sugar
Pinch of salt

FOR THE MEATBALLS:

1 slice of bread, crusts removed
1 pound (455 g) ground duck
1 egg
1 teaspoon salt

FOR THE SAUCE:

5 whole cloves
2 bay leaves
1 cinnamon stick
½ teaspoon fenugreek seeds
1 teaspoon fennel seeds
2 large onions, sliced
½ teaspoon turmeric
2 teaspoons chili powder
1 teaspoon ground coriander
1 teaspoon ground cumin
½ teaspoon salt
1 can (14 ounces, or 390 g) coconut milk
Half of a lime

FOR SERVING:

Cooked jasmine rice

* Soak the minced onions in cold water for 1 hour to draw some of the bite from them. Drain the onions and dry before adding the tomato paste, chili powder, cumin, sugar, and salt. Let rest for 1 hour before serving. If this sits for a day or two, the flavors get even better.

* Run the slice of bread under running water until it is wet. Squeeze out the excess water, like a sponge, and then put the paste into a mixing bowl. Mix the ground duck into the bread with the egg and salt. Using wet hands, roll them into bite-size balls.

* In a pan with a lid, fry the meatballs until the outside is seared all over. If there is enough fat in your duck meat, you shouldn't need to add any oil. Do add some if needed. Remove the meatballs to a plate.

* There should be about 2 tablespoons (28 ml) of oil in the same pan. Add vegetable oil if it needs more. Over medium-low heat, fry the cloves, bay leaves, cinnamon, fenugreek, and fennel seeds. After 30 seconds, add the onion and stir to coat with oil. Put the lid on for 2 to 3 minutes while cooking. Remove the lid and add the turmeric, chili powder, coriander, cumin, and salt. If the spices stick to the bottom, add a little water.

* Return the meatballs to the pan and stir to coat. Cook everything together for 10 minutes. Add the coconut milk and increase the heat so that it comes just to a boil. Then cover the pan, turn the heat to low, and cook for another 10 minutes. Check once to make sure things are not sticking to the bottom of the pan. The meatballs should be cooked through and tender. If the gravy is too thin, cook for a few minutes without the lid. There should be just enough gravy to coat the meatballs, not much more.

* Squeeze the juice from half a lime to finish. Serve with the spicy onions and white jasmine rice.

3

Fish Balls

Fish balls are quite common around the world, especially in coastal regions. Fish is transformed from the usual fillet into a darling, mild-flavored, delicate morsel. You could positively forget it is made of fish.

If you don't like the texture of fish, try it in a ball, because it changes the texture entirely. Nearly all seaside populations of the globe make their fish balls light and fluffy, except Asia, where the preference is for springy and chewy fish balls.

Fish balls are a good way to use bits of fish that didn't make it into the fillet cut. Buy the freshest fish you can. It is often possible to buy less expensive end cuts of fish perfect for chopping up; just ask your fishmonger.

CHINA } # CRUNCHY WILD SHRIMP BALLS

Yield: *24 medium fish balls; 4 to 6 servings*

1 pound (455 g) raw shrimp, peeled and deveined
4 or 5 water chestnuts
1 teaspoon salt
½ teaspoon sugar
¼ teaspoon black pepper
1 teaspoon sesame oil
1 tablespoon (15 ml) rice wine, sake, or white vermouth
1 tablespoon (8 g) cornstarch or (12 g) tapioca starch
1 package (6 ounces, or 170 g) of wonton wrappers
Canola oil, for frying
Sweet chili sauce, for dipping

● Place the shrimp, water chestnuts, salt, sugar, pepper, sesame oil, and rice wine into a food processor. Turn it on for about 30 seconds, until the ingredients become a very smooth paste. Once smooth, add the cornstarch and pulse to incorporate it. Chill the shrimp in the work bowl for 15 minutes in the fridge.

● With half of the package of wonton wrappers, slice straight downward, cutting them into neat ribbons, only ¼ inch (6 mm) wide.

● Spread the wonton wrapper ribbons in a wide pile on a flat surface. Form the shrimp paste into balls the size of ping-pong balls, using 2 spoons or wet hands. Place the shrimp ball on the wonton ribbon pile. Roll it around so the ribbons cover the ball all over. It may be a little wild looking, and that is okay.

● Deep-fry the shrimp balls in 2 inches (5 cm) of oil in a Dutch oven or a wok. Make sure the oil is hot, 350°F (180°C); the balls should cook in 2 to 3 minutes. Drain on newspapers or paper towels for a few minutes. Serve with the sweet chili sauce.

SPAIN

} **SALTED CODFISH FRITTERS**

Buñelos de Bacala

Yield: *25 large fish balls; 3 to 4 servings*

1 pound (455 g) dried salt cod
1 bay leaf
2 russet potatoes, peeled and small dice
    (1 pound [455 g])
2 tablespoons (28 ml) olive oil
½ cup (63 g) all-purpose flour
4 eggs, divided
¼ cup (15 g) chopped parsley
4 cloves of garlic, pressed
½ teaspoon fresh ground black pepper
Pinch of salt
Safflower oil, for frying

SERVING SUGGESTION:

Garlic aioli

- Freshen the salt cod the day before. Rinse any dry salt off under running water. Place the fish in a bowl and cover with cool water. Soak this way for 24 hours, changing the water at least 4 times. This extracts most of the salt from the fish.

- Put the cod and bay leaf in a pot and cover with water. Heat to just below a boil and cook for about 10 minutes until the fish is flaky. Avoid boiling the water as it will make the fish spongy. Remove the fish pieces to a bowl or plate. Flake the fish with a fork or your fingers so it is in small pieces. Remove any bones you happen to find.

- To the same water, add the chopped potato. Boil the potato till fork tender, about 5 to 7 minutes, and remove the bay leaf. The potatoes cooking in the same water will soak up some of the great flavors. Drain the potatoes in a colander, return to the warm pan, and mash very well. Add the potatoes to the bowl of flaked fish.

- In the same pot, heat the water and olive oil to a boil. Turn off the heat, dump in all the flour at once, and stir like mad with a wooden spoon. It will be like a lumpy slurry; stir to cool it down just a bit. Add 1 egg, beating rapidly with the wooden spoon until it is incorporated. Repeat in the same manner with the other eggs, beating after each addition. The batter will have most of the lumps worked out by now.

- Add the mashed potato, flaked cod, parsley, garlic, pepper, and salt. Mix it up very well; it will stiffen up more as the batter cools. The batter can be made ahead up to this point.

- To deep-fry the fritters, heat at least 2 inches (5 cm) of oil to 350°F (180°C). If you don't have a thermometer to check, a cube of white bread should turn golden in 60 seconds or less. Using 2 spoons or an ice cream scoop, drop 4 to 5 scoops into the hot oil. Turn the balls over once during cooking. They will be a deep golden brown and cooked through in about 3 minutes. Remove them to drain on newspaper or paper towels. Shower with a sprinkle of salt. Repeat with the remaining batter. Eat while hot!

- Often these fritters are served as a tapas dish with garlic aioli (page 72).

CUBA

} **FISH HASH BALLS**

Yield: *30 large fish balls; 4 to 6 servings*

1 cup (235 ml) milk
3 slices of bread, crusts removed
2 pounds (900 g) fish fillets, like snapper or tilapia
1 small onion, grated
1 teaspoon chopped parsley
1 hard-boiled egg, chopped
1 teaspoon salt
¼ teaspoon black pepper
About 1 cup (235 ml) oil for frying, canola, peanut, or corn oil

SERVING SUGGESTIONS:

Lemon wedges
Cooked rice
Green salad

* Put the milk and bread into a bowl to soak together.

* Fill a saucepan halfway with water. Bring to a simmer with a pinch of salt. Poach the fish in the water. Drop it in and allow it to cook without boiling for about 5 minutes until it flakes when touched with a spoon.

* Remove the fish to a bowl. Add the onion, parsley, and hard-boiled egg. Mash everything together to mix. Add the milk-soaked bread, salt, and pepper. Mash to combine everything very well.

* Heat ¼ inch (6 mm) of oil in a skillet for frying the fish balls. When it is nice and hot, scoop the fish into balls with 2 spoons. Cook in the hot oil, 2 to 3 minutes per side, until golden brown all over. Remove to drain on paper towels.

* Eat hot, served with lemon wedges, rice, and fresh green salad.

USA

} **FRIED FISH BALLS**

with Grilled Pineapple Salsa

Yield: *24 large fish balls; 4 servings*

FOR THE SALSA:

2 cups (330 g) fresh pineapple

2 medium fresh tomatoes, cut in half, seeds removed

1 medium red onion

½ of a jalapeño pepper, seeds removed

¼ cup (4 g) chopped cilantro

½ teaspoon salt

¼ teaspoon black pepper

1 ounce (28 ml) lime juice

FOR THE FISH BALLS:

1½ pounds (680 g) fresh white fish

1¼ teaspoons salt

Pinch of black pepper

1 large onion (about 1½ cups [240 g] diced)

1 tablespoon (15 ml) vegetable oil

4 tablespoons (31 g) all-purpose flour

1 teaspoon baking powder

3 tablespoons (45 ml) buttermilk (or milk)

1 tablespoon (4 g) chopped parsley

2 tablespoons (23 g) chopped canned roasted red peppers

¼ teaspoon paprika

Roughly 2 cups (475 ml) vegetable oil for frying

* Grill the pineapple slices on a griddle pan or an outdoor grill. They are done when the grill leaves dark golden lines where the sugar caramelizes. Dice the pineapple, tomatoes, onion, jalapeño, and cilantro. This can be done in a food processor; however, be cautious to not overmix it to a purée. Mix in a bowl with the salt, pepper, and lime juice. Cover for 30 minutes to meld the flavors. Well covered, it can be kept for a week in the fridge.

* Chop the fish into small pieces, roughly the size of a green pea. Place in a large bowl with the salt and pepper. Sauté the diced onion in the vegetable oil until tender. Add the flour, baking powder, buttermilk, parsley, roasted red peppers, paprika, and cooked onion to the fish. Use 2 spoons to toss and mix the fish well.

* Heat enough oil to come 1½ to 2 inches (3.8 to 5 cm) up the sides of a high-sided pan with a heavy bottom, suitable for deep-frying. Frying in small batches is the best way to keep the oil at the correct temperature. Bring the oil up to 350°F (180°C). If you don't have a thermometer to check, a cube of white bread should turn golden in 60 seconds or less. Have paper towels or newspaper ready to drain the fried fish balls.

* Using 2 spoons, form round balls of the fish mixture. Drop them from the spoon into the hot oil. Avoid crowding the frying balls. As they turn golden in the oil, turn them over to ensure both sides are cooked. Use a slotted spoon to remove the fish balls to drain on paper towels as they turn a deep golden brown. Sprinkle with some sea salt. Repeat with all the chopped fish. Eat at once with the salsa!

AUSTRALIA

BEER-BATTERED FISH BALLS

with Chili Dipping Sauce

Yield: *24 large fish balls; 4 servings*

FOR THE FISH BALLS:

1½ cups (188 g) all-purpose flour plus
  3 tablespoons (23 g), and more for
  dredging, divided

1½ teaspoons salt, divided

1¾ cups (410 ml) pale lager beer

½ teaspoon black pepper

1½ pounds (680 g) white fish such as tilapia

FOR THE CHILI SAUCE:

2 tablespoons (32 g) chunky chili paste

1 to 2 shallots, minced

1 tablespoon (15 ml) rice vinegar

1 teaspoon sugar

* In a bowl, mix 1½ cups (188 g) flour with ½ teaspoon salt. Slowly pour in the beer while whisking. Mix until the batter is nearly smooth. Don't overwork it, some lumps are okay. Let it rest for 15 minutes to fully hydrate.

* To make the chili sauce, mix the chili paste, shallots, rice vinegar, sugar, and a pinch of salt together well.

* Use a large chopping knife to mince the fish or employ a food processor, pulsing a few times and stopping before it is puréed. It is nice to have some chunks of fish. Season the fish with pepper and 1 teaspoon of salt and mix in the 3 tablespoons (23 g) of flour.

* Turn on the oven to 200°F (93°C) to keep the balls warm after frying. Dump a handful of flour into a shallow bowl for dredging the balls before they go into the batter.

* Right before frying, form some of the puréed fish into 1½-inch (3.8 cm) balls with a spring-loaded ice cream scoop or two spoons. Drop them into the bowl of flour, dredge the balls in flour by rolling them around, lift out from below with a fork, and shake off the excess. Dip each in the beer batter and let the excess drip off. Add the battered fish balls to the hot oil and fry. Turn once or twice until golden brown on all sides and the fish is cooked through, about 5 minutes. Remove the fish balls and drain on newspaper. Sprinkle with salt. Keep warm until serving with chili sauce.

Note:

This is an Aussie fusion of fish and chips, inspired by British and Southeast Asian cuisine. Serve on toothpicks at a party or throw some potato wedges in the frying oil while you are at it for a fish and chip treat!

INDIA

STEAMED SPICY MUSSEL BALLS

of Mumbai

Yield: *12 medium fish balls; 4 servings*

FOR THE MUSSEL BALLS:

1 cup shelled mussels (250 g) or meats from about 25 mussels

1 teaspoon ground coriander

¼ teaspoon turmeric

1 teaspoon chili powder

2 tablespoons (28 ml) coconut or olive oil

2 onions, diced

1 tomato, diced

4 green chiles

5 cloves of garlic, crushed

1 piece ginger (½ inch [1.3 cm]), grated

½ teaspoon cumin seeds

Small handful of cilantro leaves, chopped

½ teaspoon salt

1½ cups (180 g) chickpea flour, or (188 g) all-purpose wheat flour

¼ teaspoon baking soda

1 tablespoon (15 ml) water

FOR THE SEASONING:

1 tablespoon (15 ml) sesame oil

1 tablespoon (8 g) sesame seeds

1 tablespoon (11 g) mustard seeds

1 bay leaf

• Marinate the mussels in the coriander, turmeric, and chili powder for 10 to 20 minutes. Fry them in hot coconut oil until cooked through, about 1 minute. Remove and roughly chop the mussels. Set aside.

• Using the same pan and coconut oil, sauté the onion on medium heat for about 5 minutes to soften it. Add the tomato, chiles, garlic, ginger, and cumin seeds. When it has turned fragrant and things have softened, turn off the heat. Return the chopped mussels and add the cilantro to the onion mixture. Add the salt and more spice if desired.

• In the pan, or a bowl if your pan is too small, mix the chickpea flour and baking soda into the mussel mixture. Let it sit for 15 minutes. The flour will absorb the liquid and juices. Knead the dough after it rests. If the dough is very sticky, add more flour. If it is dry, add the tablespoon (15 ml) of water and more if necessary. The goal is to have a dough that sticks together and is moist but not gummy or sticky.

• Put a little oil on clean hands. Roll 2-inch-wide (5 cm) balls of the dough. Make them neat and even. Place them on a steamer basket or plate.

• To steam the balls, boil 1 inch (2.5 cm) of water in the bottom of a lidded pan. There are many devices for steaming; use a bamboo or metal basket steamer, an egg poaching machine, a rice maker, or a pan sitting on a trivet inside a larger pot. Whichever tool you use, steam the balls for 15 minutes. Remove them from the steamer.

• To saturate the outside of the balls with flavor, a technique called tempering is employed. In a clean pan that can accommodate the steamed balls, heat the sesame oil. When hot, throw in the sesame seeds, mustard seeds, and bay leaf. The seeds will pop and maybe sputter. They will color quickly. In seconds they will be toasted. Now add the steamed balls into the hot oil. Shake them around so they pick up the sesame seeds and the flavor. Remove the bay leaf.

• Serve right away. They are nice as a midafternoon snack with tea or coffee.

Mussels

} # KERALA RED CURRY
with Fish Balls

Yield: *8 large fish balls; 2 servings*

FOR THE FISH BALLS:

½ pound (225 g) fish
4 whole peppercorns
1 inch (2.5 cm) fresh ginger, sliced
¼ cup (40 g) onion, roughly chopped
1 green chile, sliced in half
1 to 2 cups (235 to 475 ml) water
1 slice of bread, crusts removed
1 egg yolk
¼ teaspoon salt
¼ teaspoon black pepper
1 tablespoon (8 g) all-purpose flour

FOR THE CURRY:

1½ tablespoons (23 ml) safflower oil
¼ teaspoon fenugreek seeds
¼ cup (40 g) sliced shallots
½ cup (90 g) chopped tomato (fresh or canne without juice)
1 large clove of garlic
1 inch (2.5 cm) fresh ginger
¼ teaspoon turmeric
1 tablespoon (8 g) chili powder
Coconut milk (optional)

FOR SERVING:

Cooked rice or flatbread

* Place the fish, peppercorns, ginger, onion and chile into a small saucepan. Pour the water over the fish, just to cover it. Put the saucepan on medium-high heat and simmer for about 3 minutes until cooked through. It will flake easily. Carefully remove the fish into a mixing bowl. The aromatic flavorings should be left in the water. Reserve the poaching liquid to use in the curry sauce.

* Flake the fish with a fork into small pieces. Dunk the bread slice into the warm poaching liquid. Wring out the excess liquid and crumble the bread into the fish, breaking it into small pieces. Add the egg yolk, salt, pepper, and flour. Mix well with a fork and set aside.

* In a medium saucepan, heat the oil until shimmering. Toss in the fenugreek seeds. They will crackle in the oil and release a fragrance. Allow them to cook for about 2 minutes until the smell changes and has a toasted, nutty quality to it. Add the shallots, cooking on low until soft and pale, about 4 minutes.

* Meanwhile, make the curry paste. Purée the tomato, garlic, ginger, turmeric, and chili powder in a food processor. The puree will be deep red and smooth. Pour the purée over the cooked shallot. Raise the heat to extract more flavor from the curry paste. Look for it to boil at the edges of the pot. Stir slowly for 30 seconds.

* Strain the fish poaching liquid into the curry paste: 1 cup (235 ml) if you want a thick curry and the entire amount for a more soupy sauce. Bring to a boil and turn down the heat to a simmer. Be advised that the curry on its own is spicy. Keep the sauce at a low simmer.

* Returning to the fish mixture, it should be squeezed into balls with 1 hand. Make about 8 balls the size of ping-pong balls, about 2 inches (5 cm). Drop each into the curry as it is made. Once they are all in the sauce, the tops may still poke out above the sauce. Shake the pan to coat them in curry sauce. Simmer on the lowest setting for 15 minutes. Keep warm until eating.

* Serve with rice or with flatbread such as naan. If the curry sauce is too spicy for your palate, stir a half can of coconut milk into the sauce.

Tip:

This curry is so flavorful it will pair with nearly any fish you put in it! Flaky white fish, salmon, sardines, trout, mahi mahi, or kingfish (popular in Kerala) would be great. Support sustainable fishing practices by choosing what is abundant and local near your home.

WEST AFRICA

} **SPICY FISH BALLS**

in Tomato Vegetable Stew

Yield: *20 small fish balls; 3 to 4 servings*

FOR THE FISH BALLS:

1 pound (455 g) fish, such as snapper, tilapia, or bluefish

½ teaspoon salt

¼ teaspoon black pepper

1 small onion

2 to 3 fresh chile peppers to taste

3 cloves of garlic

1 tablespoon (16 g) peanut butter

½ cup (120 ml) peanut oil, or vegetable for frying

FOR THE STEW:

2 fresh tomatoes, chopped

1 tablespoon (16g) tomato paste

1 large onion, minced

2 cloves of garlic, sliced

1 teaspoon black pepper

Fresh chiles, to taste

Pinch of salt

2 cups (475 ml) vegetable or fish stock

2 carrots, sliced

1 sweet potato, large dice

1 cup (90 g) sliced cabbage

FOR SERVING:

Cooked rice or couscous (page 27)

* Remove any bones and skin from the fish. Put the pieces of fish along with the salt and pepper into the food processor. Blend so the fish is minced so small it will be a chunky paste. Put the fish in a bowl. Mince the onion, chiles, and garlic in the food processor as well. These can all be minced by hand if you don't have a food processor. Combine them with the fish.

* It is easiest to mix with one hand, folding the fish over itself. Mix the onions and chiles in well and add in the peanut butter, mixing until it is all combined.

* Using wet or oiled hands, roll compact 1-inch (2.5 cm) balls of the fish mixture. Set them onto a plate to await cooking.

* In a wok or pan with tall sides, heat the oil until a test piece bubbles like crazy when it touches the oil. Cook the fish balls in batches so as to not crowd the oil. Turn them over a few times while cooking and remove when browned on the outside. After cooking all the fish balls, set them aside.

* To make the tomato sauce, remove all but 3 tablespoons (45 ml) of oil from the pan. Add the chopped tomatoes, tomato paste, onion, garlic, black pepper, chiles, and a pinch of salt. If your tomatoes are more dry than juicy, add a few tablespoons (45 to 60 ml) of water while it simmers. Cover and let simmer on medium low for 5 to 10 minutes. The sauce will be thick and red, and the oil will have floated to the top.

* Take the lid off and add the stock, carrot, sweet potato, and cabbage. Also add the fish balls. Cover and simmer for 15 minutes on medium-low heat so the vegetables cook through. Add salt if necessary. Serve over rice or couscous.

Note:

The entire stew can come together within an hour. Adjust the spice, change out the vegetables, and make it your own.

CARIBBEAN

FISH AND YUCCA DUMPLINGS
with Callaloo

Yield: *12 large fish balls; 4 servings*

FOR THE CALLALOO:

1 can (14 ounces, or 390 g) coconut milk

1 small yellow onion, diced

1 clove of garlic, crushed

15 to 20 fresh okra, or 10 ounces (280 g) frozen

1 hot fresh chile, seeds removed, chopped

1 pound (455 g) fresh spinach, or 10 ounces (280 g) frozen

½ teaspoon salt

¼ teaspoon black pepper

FOR THE YUCCA DUMPLINGS:

1½ pounds (680 g) frozen yucca

¼ cup (60 ml) peanut oil, or safflower

1 onion, diced

2 cloves of garlic, crushed

¼ teaspoon ground cumin

Pinch of chili powder

1 teaspoon salt

1 pound (455 g) fish fillets, snapper, or tilapia

- Make the callaloo in a large pan. Combine the coconut milk, onion, garlic, okra, chile, spinach, salt, and pepper. Bring to a boil and then turn it all down to a simmer and cook on low for 20 minutes. Take off the heat.

- Using a hand blender or countertop blender, purée the callaloo until the vegetables are puréed. There should be enough liquid to blend easily. Add some water or vegetable stock if necessary.

- To prepare the yucca, simmer it in a pot of boiling water for 30 minutes until fork tender, just as if you were boiling potatoes. Drain and return to the pot. Using a sturdy spoon or masher, coarsely mash the yucca so there are still many lumps. Set aside to cool until easy to handle.

- Heat the oil in a skillet. When hot, add the onion, garlic, spices, and salt and cook until the onion is quite soft and tender. Add the fish fillets right on top of the onion. Cook for 3 minutes on each side, just so it cooks through and flakes easily. Don't worry about being neat, as it will all be mashed up soon.

- Scoop all the fish and onions into the mashed yucca. Stir it together so it is combined but there are still many lumps of fish or yucca. Taste it and add more salt if necessary. While the yucca is warm, roll it into balls. Using wet hands to roll the balls will keep the yucca nice and neat.

- Warm up the callaloo and serve it hot in soup bowls with a few yucca balls on the side and dashes of hot sauce. They are nice to eat together. Put them in the callaloo or dip them in as you eat.

Tip:

If you have leftover yucca fish balls, cook them the next day by searing them in a frying pan in a little oil. The outsides will turn golden brown and crispy.

Note:

Callaloo is a very green stew developed by West Africans living in the West Indies as slaves. It draws on culinary traditions from West Africa and has many variations among the Caribbean islands. It is usually made with the leaves of the cassava plant, but spinach works for all of us who don't live in the tropics. Callaloo is the national dish of Trinidad and Tobago and is a great way to eat greens.

MOROCCO

MOROCCAN CHARD AND CHICKPEAS FISH BALL TAGINE

Yield: 24 small fish balls; 4 to 5 servings

FOR THE FISH BALLS:

1 pound (455 g) cod or other firm fish, such as red snapper

½ cup (120 ml) chermoula sauce (page 90, Chermoula Chicken Boulettes)

⅓ cup (40 g) chickpea flour

¼ cup (60 ml) milk

1 teaspoon salt

FOR THE TAGINE:

2 tablespoons (28 ml) olive oil

1 small onion, sliced

1 clove of garlic, minced

1 teaspoon turmeric

1 teaspoon sweet paprika

1 pinch of cayenne pepper

About 12 leaves of Swiss chard or kale, deveined, sliced crosswise into narrow ribbons

2 cans (15 ounces, or 425 g each) chickpeas, drained, rinsed (about 3 cups [720 g])

1 can (28 ounces, or 805 g) whole peeled tomatoes

½ of a preserved lemon, chopped, or zest of 2 lemons

¾ teaspoon salt

FOR SERVING:

Couscous, prepared according to box instructions

- Chop the fish into fine pieces: using a food processor, pulse it about 6 times. Scoop it into a bowl and mix it with the chermoula sauce to marinate for an hour in the fridge.

- Heat the olive oil in a tagine or sauté pan over medium heat. Cook the onion for nearly 10 minutes until soft and tender. Add the garlic and spices, stir, and cook until fragrant. Add the ribbons of leafy greens and chickpeas. Pour the tomato liquid into the stew and rip apart the tomatoes into bite-size pieces as they are added. Add the chopped preserved lemon and salt. Bring the entire dish to a simmer for 5 minutes, while working on the fish balls.

- Add the chickpea flour, milk, and salt to the bowl of minced fish and chermoula sauce. Mix it all well. Form quenelles of the fish mixture and drop each one on top of the simmering chickpea sauce. Immediately put the lid on and cook for 15 minutes on the lowest heat. Serve right away, bringing the dish to the table to eat with couscous.

Tip:

Tagine is the name for a stew and the vessel it is cooked in, a glazed earthenware dish, like a deep pie plate, with a tall, cone-shaped lid with a small hole in it. To replicate the effect with Western kitchenware, use a Dutch oven or a heavy sauté pan with a tight-fitting lid. The tagine is traditionally placed in hot coals to cook; a very low setting on the stove, using a diffuser if necessary, will do the same thing. A tagine makes a beautiful serving dish when the stew is presented at the table.

TUNISIA

} **MONKFISH BALLS**

in a Tagine of Tomato, Olives, and Preserved Lemon

Yield: *24 medium fish balls; 4 to 5 servings*

FOR THE MONKFISH BALLS:

1 pound (455 g) monkfish
½ cup (120 ml) chermoula sauce (page 90,
  Chermoula Chicken Boulettes)
⅓ cup (38 g) bread crumbs
1 teaspoon salt

FOR THE TAGINE:

3 tablespoons (45 ml) olive oil
1 yellow onion, sliced
4 cloves of garlic, thinly sliced
¼ cup (60 ml) water
3 cups (450 g) cherry tomatoes
½ cup (85 g) cured black olives, rinsed
½ teaspoon black pepper
1 tablespoon (6 g) minced preserved lemon
  (See Tip.)
1 handful of chopped herbs (such as parsley,
  cilantro, or oregano)

SERVING SUGGESTIONS:

Flatbread
Cooked rice

- Puree the monkfish using a food processor: pulse it until it is a thick paste or chop until finely minced. Mix in the chermoula sauce, bread crumbs, and salt. Chill for 1 hour to allow the flavors to marinate.

- Heat the olive oil in the base of a tagine or sauté pan with a tight-fitting lid. Keep the heat on low and cook the onion, garlic, and water, covered, for about 8 minutes. They will become soft. Add the tomatoes, olives, black pepper, and preserved lemon. Cook covered for 10 minutes until softened.

- Form small 1½-inch (3.8 cm) balls of the puréed fish, using 2 spoons. Place into the tagine on top of the tomatoes and olives. Replace the cover once all the balls are in place. Cook for 15 minutes on low heat. The tagine creates a slow cooking environment that is a mixture of braising and steaming. This results in very tender food, highly saturated with flavor.

- Remove the tagine from the heat. Sprinkle chopped herbs over everything. Serve it in its dish at the table, as it is beautiful this way. Flatbread or rice would be nice to accompany the main dish.

Tip:

Preserved lemons are an indispensable ingredient in North African cuisine. You can find them in well-stocked groceries and Middle Eastern markets. A simple replacement for preserved lemon is lemon zest and a squeeze of lemon juice.

USA

SAN FRANCISCO CRAB BALL CHOWDER

Yield: *20 small fish balls; 4 to 5 servings*

FOR THE CHOWDER:

1 pound (455 g) mussels

2 tablespoons (28 ml) olive oil

2 medium onions, diced

1 green bell pepper, seeded and diced

1 stalk of celery, diced

3 cloves of garlic, smashed and sliced

⅓ cup (80 ml) dry white wine

3 cups (700 ml) fish stock or water

1 bay leaf

½ cup (77 g) sweet corn

4 new potatoes, diced

¼ teaspoon salt

¼ teaspoon black pepper

1 piece kombu (dried kelp) roughly 7 x 2 inches (18 x 5 cm) in size (See Note.)

½ of a can (28 ounces, or 785 g) canned whole peeled tomatoes

Handful of chopped parsley

FOR THE CRAB BALLS:

8 ounces (225 g) crab meat (Fresh is best. Canned works too, but check the weight.)

1 egg

½ teaspoon sea salt

¼ teaspoon black pepper

½ cup (60 g) bread crumbs or (50 g) panko

2 tablespoons (28 ml) milk

2 tablespoons (12 g) chopped scallions

½ tablespoon (5 g) dry mustard

Dash of hot sauce (optional)

¼ cup (35 g) cornmeal

½ teaspoon Old Bay seasoning

Nearly ¼ cup (60 ml) sunflower oil, or canola

* Clean the mussels by filling a bowl with cold water and allowing the mussels to rest in it for 15 to 20 minutes. Discard any with broken shells. Remove any beards which remain on the mussels.

* In a large soup pot, heat the olive oil and sauté the onions, bell pepper, and celery. Stir frequently. After about 6 minutes, add the garlic. Once the garlic is fragrant, deglaze the pan with the white wine; scrape up any brown bits on the bottom of the pan while the wine boils. After a minute, the alcohol will cook off. Add the stock or water, bay leaf, corn, potatoes, salt, and pepper. Cut the kombu into strips with kitchen shears and add to the soup. The canned peeled tomatoes can be torn apart with your hands into smaller pieces; add half the juice in the can to the soup. Bring the soup to a boil and then turn the heat to low and simmer for 1 hour for maximum flavor.

* While the soup is simmering, make the crab balls. Drain the crab well and place into a mixing bowl. Check for sharp pieces of shell. Add the egg, seasoning, bread crumbs, milk, scallions, dry mustard, and hot sauce (if using). Mix well. Pour the cornmeal into a shallow dish and mix the Old Bay into the cornmeal. Using a small scoop or spoons, form 1-inch (2.5 cm) balls. Roll them in the seasoned cornmeal and place on a sheet of waxed paper to await cooking. Repeat with all the crab mixture.

* The crab balls can be baked, but the flavor falls flat in comparison to the pan-fried version. (See Tip.) Heat a cast-iron skillet, coating the bottom with a generous slick of vegetable oil. When the oil shimmers, it is time to place the crab balls in. Avoid crowding the pan; it is helpful to have enough room to roll the balls around. Fry all sides until toasted brown; this may take about 6 minutes. Remove to a paper towel to drain any extra oil. Keep the fried balls warm in a low oven at 150°F (66°C) until ready to serve.

* Serve in soup bowls, topped with fresh chopped parsley and the fried crab balls. If the balls have time to absorb the soup, they lose all their crispness, so add them on top right before eating.

Note:

Kombu, or dried kelp, is a seaweed and can be purchased at most grocery stores. Look for it with the international foods or in the natural foods aisle. It is hard when dry, but in a soup it turns soft and when cut into small pieces, will blend in with other vegetables. Seaweeds add wonderful flavor to soups and act as a thickener also! They are high in minerals and vitamins. So even if you don't enjoy swimming with seaweed, it is really good to eat!

Tip:

If you would rather bake the crab balls, dunk them in a beaten egg before rolling them in cornmeal. This will help the crust become crunchy in the oven.

KOREA } # FISH BALL AND NOODLE SOUP

Yield: *4 large fish balls; 2 to 3 servings*

FOR THE FISH BALLS:

10 ounces (280 g) fresh fish fillet (snapper, grouper, dory, or pike)
1 tablespoon (8 g) tapioca starch
1 tablespoon (15 ml) water
½ teaspoon salt
½ teaspoon black pepper

FOR THE SOUP:

1 liter (1 quart) fish or vegetable stock
1 piece of fresh ginger (½ inch [1.3 cm]), minced
1 scallion, cut in 4 pieces
1 carrot, sliced
4 or 5 mushrooms, sliced
1 head of bok choy, sliced
Egg or udon noodles, for 2 servings
Scallions
Cilantro
1 teaspoon soy sauce

- To make the fish balls, put the fish in a food processor and pulse until it is smooth. Make a slurry of the starch and water. Add the salt, pepper, and slurry. A tablespoon or two (15 to 28 ml) more of water can be added to help process it into a paste. Without a food processor, it can be done the old-fashioned way: on a sturdy cutting board with the back side of a knife. Using the back side of a chopping knife minces the fish but also flattens it in a way, tenderizing it. Chop the fish until it is a complete paste and no longer resembles fish at all. Remember to add in the slurry, but you shouldn't need any extra water.

- Have ready a cutting board or a large bowl to work from. Gather up the fish paste, holding it with both hands. Bring it up to the level of your face and then slap it down into the bowl or board. Repeat, lifting the paste up and throwing the paste down, many times. Some people say about 60 times, but you could get away with 20. The goal is that the paste should pass out of a mushy stage and turn wobbly, like gelatin.

- Make ready a large bowl of cold water. Form into 2-inch-wide (5 cm) balls. The traditional way is to take a lot of paste in one hand and a spoon in the other. Squeeze the paste in your fist so that it extrudes in the hole made by the base of the thumb and first finger. Use the spoon to slice off the ball. Place the newly made balls in the bowl of cold water, so they don't stick to anything.

- To make the soup, bring the stock to a boil in a pot. Add the ginger, scallion, carrot, and mushrooms. Simmer for 15 minutes. Add the bok choy to the soup and cook another 3 minutes.

- Bring a pot of water to a boil. Cook the noodles in the water for as long as directed on the package. Pull out of the pot and rinse under cold water. Shake off the excess water. Set aside.

- In the same pot of boiling water, cook the fish balls. Place them into boiling water and keep it at a simmer. They will float when cooked through.

- Dunk the noodles into the hot soup to reheat them. Remove them and divide between the large soup bowls. Put some vegetables and fish balls in each one and top with broth. Top with the scallions, cilantro, and a dash of soy sauce.

Notes:

Vendors of fish cakes and fish balls are a common sight on Korean streets. They sell them as soup or on sticks with a dipping sauce. This coastal tradition uses all bits of the fish; the little bits that are left over after the fillet is removed can be scraped off with a spoon and gathered for fish balls.

A desirable quality in Asian fish balls is a certain springiness. To get this bounce, use the freshest fish you can, choosing a medium-firm fish. If purchasing fish balls in the frozen section of Asian grocery stores, look for ones with a high percentage of fish and few additives.

USA

CATFISH HUSH PUPPIES

with Coleslaw

Yield: *20 large fish balls; 3 servings*

FOR THE COLESLAW:

1 head of green cabbage, shredded

1 to 2 carrots, shredded

3 tablespoons (42 g) mayonnaise

1 to 2 tablespoons (15 to 28 ml) apple cider vinegar

½ teaspoon celery seed

1 teaspoon Dijon mustard

½ teaspoon black pepper

1 teaspoon salt

FOR THE HUSH PUPPIES:

1 pound (455 g) catfish, chopped small

⅔ cup (160 ml) buttermilk

1 cup (140 g) cornmeal

½ cup (63 g) all-purpose flour

1 teaspoon baking soda

1 teaspoon salt

1 teaspoon sugar

¼ teaspoon cayenne pepper

¼ teaspoon black pepper

1 egg, beaten lightly

Peanut or canola oil, for frying

* To make the slaw, mix everything up in a bowl. Add more mayo if you have a lot of cabbage. Knead it together and set aside.

* The catfish should be chopped small, into ¼-inch (6-mm) pieces. Put it in a bowl with the buttermilk. Set aside.

* In a mixing bowl, whisk together the cornmeal, flour, baking soda, salt, sugar, and cayenne pepper.

* Heat 2 to 3 inches (5 to 7.5 cm) of oil in a Dutch oven or heavy pan with high sides. Bring the temperature up to 375°F (190°C). Get ready a tray with newspaper or paper towels to drain the hush puppies.

* Add the egg, buttermilk, and fish to the dry ingredients. Stir around until you have a thick batter.

* Use a small ice cream scoop or 2 spoons to scoop out portions of batter. They should be only 1 to 2 tablespoons (15 to 28 g) each. Drop each one into the fryer. Fill the pot without crowding it; turn them once as they fry. The hush puppies cook very quickly, in just 2 minutes. Remove with a slotted spoon and drain on the newspaper.

* Serve right away with the coleslaw and ketchup.

Note:

A true American Southern meal is fried hush puppies, cornmeal-crusted catfish, coleslaw, and ketchup. Usually the catfish and cornmeal hush puppy are separate things, but they are so good cooked together, so why not?

GERMANY

} # BAKED FISH BALLS
with Frankfurt Green Sauce

Yield: *20 large fish balls; 4 servings*

FOR THE FISH BALLS:

1 pound (455 g) pike fish fillets, (or other white fish like walleye, tilapia, or orange roughy)

2 large eggs (cold)

¼ cup (30 g) plain fine bread crumbs

¾ teaspoon salt

¼ teaspoon white pepper

⅛ teaspoon freshly grated nutmeg

1 cup (235 ml) heavy cream, very cold

FOR THE GREEN SAUCE

2 hard-boiled eggs

½ cup (115 g) sour cream

½ cup (60 ml) buttermilk or yogurt

3½ ounces (100 g) mixed fresh herbs, about 5 packed cups (chervil, watercress, parsley, sorrel, chives, borage, or salad burnet)

1 tablespoon (11 g) mustard

1 tablespoon (15 ml) dill pickle juice

Salt and black pepper, to taste

SERVING OPTIONS:

Bolied potatoes

- In a food processor, purée the fish for 20 seconds. Stop when smooth; it will be very thick. Add the eggs, bread crumbs, salt, white pepper, and nutmeg and pulse about 6 times to combine. Slowly pour the cream down the feed tube while the processor is running. Continue to purée for about 15 seconds until the fish is very smooth. Transfer the mixture to a bowl, cover with plastic, and let it rest and chill for 30 minutes in the fridge.

- Meanwhile, make the green sauce. Split the hard-boiled eggs into yolks and whites. Chop the whites into a small dice and set aside. Put the egg yolks into a mixing bowl. Break up the yolks with a fork and then combine the sour cream and buttermilk into the yolk. Remove the thick stems from the herbs, using only the tender leaves and stems. Chop them very fine; for some reason they taste a bit better if chopped by hand. Stir all the herbs into the sauce. Once they are all incorporated, add the mustard, dill pickle juice, egg whites, salt, and pepper to taste. Chill until served.

- Butter the bottom of a 9 x 12-inch (23 x 30 cm) baking dish. Form the cold fish mixture into balls the size of an egg. Set each one in the baking dish so there is room around each one. The balls can be formed with wet hands or use 2 soup spoons to form quenelles. Cover the baking dish with aluminum foil. Place in a preheated 325°F (170°C, or gas mark 3) oven. Bake until firm, about 30 to 40 minutes.

- Serve the green sauce on the plate next to the fish balls, perhaps with some boiled potatoes and sparkling apple cider for a real Frankfurt feast!

Mixed fresh herbs

SCANDINAVIA

} **FISKEBOLLER**

Yield: *12 large fish balls; 2 to 3 servings*

FOR THE FISKEBOLLER:

1 pound (455 g) haddock or cod fillet, all bones removed
1 teaspoon salt
½ teaspoon white pepper
1 tablespoon (12 g) potato starch (See Tip.)
½ cup (120 ml) milk
2 egg whites

FOR THE WHITE SAUCE:

1¼ cups (295 ml) milk
2 tablespoons (28 g) butter
2 tablespoons (16 g) all-purpose flour
Salt and black pepper, to taste

FOR SERVING:

Steamed vegetables
Boiled potatoes

- A food processor makes the task of mixing the fiskeboller very easy and quick. Place the fish fillet in the bowl of the food processor and pulse for several seconds until the fish is a rough paste. While the machine is stopped, add the salt, white pepper, and potato starch. Pulse to mix. Turn the food processor on and pour in the milk and egg whites while it is running. Turn the machine off when the liquids are incorporated.

- Bring a wide pan of salted water to a simmer. Remove the blade from the food processor bowl. Using 2 soup spoons, form quenelles (football shapes) of the fish paste. Gently lower the fiskeboller into the simmering water with a slotted spoon. Poach for 10 minutes. Remove to a platter. Cover with aluminum foil to keep warm while making the white sauce.

- To make the white sauce, begin by heating the milk in a small pan until bubbles form at the edge or in the microwave 30 seconds at a time until it is hot to the touch. Melt the butter in a heavy-bottomed saucepan. Whisk in the flour and cook it about 2 minutes. It will bubble, but don't let it turn brown. Pour in the warm milk a little bit at a time, whisking to remove lumps. Bring to a boil and simmer for about 3 minutes. Add salt and pepper to taste. If not using the sauce immediately, place waxed paper or a splash of fresh milk over the top of the sauce to prevent a skin from forming.

- Serve with steamed fresh vegetables and boiled potatoes for a classic meal.

Tip:

Potato starch can be substituted with potato flour, arrowroot powder, or cornstarch.

Note:

Fiskeboller have a mild taste and airy texture; they almost melt in your mouth, hardly tasting of fish at all. Children will enjoy them, especially with the classic white sauce. Dill sauce or curry sauce would also go well.

GREECE

} # HERBED SWORDFISH BALLS

Psarokeftethes

Yield: *24 large fish balls; 4 servings*

8 ounces (225 g) salt cod
½ cup (120 ml) milk
1 pound (455 g) swordfish
1 cup (60 g) chopped parsley
½ cup (48 g) chopped fresh mint
2 tablespoons (8 g) fresh dill
6 to 8 cloves of garlic, minced
3 to 4 slices of stale bread, crusts removed
 (about 2 cups [60 g])
⅓ heaping cup (42 g) all-purpose flour
4 eggs
2 tablespoons (28 ml) lemon juice
2 teaspoons salt
½ teaspoon black pepper
Canola oil, for frying

- Refresh the salt cod the day before. Rinse any dry salt off under running water. Place the fish in a bowl and cover with cool water. Soak this way for 24 hours, changing the water at least 4 times. This extracts most of the salt from the fish.

- Fill a saucepan halfway with water and the milk. Bring to a simmer and add a big pinch of salt, about a tablespoon (18 g). Add the fish pieces to the simmering water. Poach for 5 to 7 minutes until fully cooked. The swordfish should be opaque all the way through, and the codfish should flake easily. Strain, discarding the poaching liquid. Return the fish to the cooking pot. Flake it using a fork, or your hands, so they are now all small pieces. Remove any bones or tough parts.

- Place the chopped herbs and garlic in a large mixing bowl. Soak the bread slices in water. When they are saturated, squeeze out the excess water and put them with the herbs. Mash the bread to a pulp with your hands or a fork, mixing well into the herbs.

- Add the flaked fish and flour into the herb-bread mixture. Stir a few times. Add the eggs, lemon juice, salt, and pepper. Beat well with a fork to combine everything.

- These can now be cooked into balls by deep-frying or as patties in a skillet. They are measurably better when deep-fried. Heat 2 inches (5 cm) of oil in a small pan with high sides to 350°F (180°C) or when a test piece bubbles violently immediately after contact with the oil. Form egg-shaped balls with 2 spoons or use an ice cream scoop, as the batter is quite loose. Drop one in the oil, flip over once golden brown on the bottom, and remove to drain on paper towels. Taste this one to ensure the fish balls don't need more pepper or salt or lemon! Once satisfied, continue to fry the remaining batter, as many portions comfortably fit in your frying oil without crowding. Drain them well on paper and keep warm in a 180°F (82°C) oven until serving.

Tip:

Don't feel you must use swordfish or salt cod; most any firm-fleshed fish would be good. Many fishmongers will have swordfish "tips," small pieces that were trimmed from the showy steaks. This is a perfect place to use these end cuts, which usually cost less per pound than the steaks.

} # NEW ENGLAND CODFISH BALLS

with Tartar Sauce

Yield: *8–12 large fish balls; 5 servings*

FOR THE TARTAR SAUCE:

1 cup (225 g) mayonnaise
⅓ cup (48 g) minced dill pickle
1 tablespoon (9 g) chopped capers
1 tablespoon (4 g) chopped parsley
1 teaspoon mustard
2 teaspoons minced shallots
2 teaspoons lemon juice

FOR THE CODFISH BALLS:

½ pound (225 g) salt cod (or fresh)
2 cups (220 g) peeled potato, cut in small dice
½ teaspoon black pepper
1 tablespoon (14 g) butter
1 egg
¼ cup (60 ml) milk or cream (unless using leftover mashed potato)

- To make the tartar sauce, make sure everything is chopped fine and mix it together with the mayonnaise.

- If using salt cod, freshen it the day before. Rinse any dry salt off under running water. Place the fish in a bowl and cover with cool water. Soak this way for 24 hours, changing the water at least 4 times.

- Take the small diced potatoes, put them in a pot, and fill it with cool water 2 inches (5 cm) above the potatoes. Bring the water and potatoes to a boil. Boil for 5 minutes, turn it down to a steady simmer, and put in the salt cod. Don't allow the water to boil again or it will make the codfish spongy. Cook until the codfish is tender and flaky, 7 to 10 minutes, and the potatoes are tender. Drain through a colander. Transfer into a bowl, add the butter, and mash it all up so the lumps are nearly gone. Mix in the egg, pepper, and cream.

- If using leftover mashed potatoes and leftover cod, simply mix them together, roughly 1 cup (225 g) cod to 2 cups (450 g) potato and add 1 egg. You shouldn't need to add butter, cream, or pepper if these things are already in your mashed potato.

- To cook the codfish balls, there are two options: browning in a skillet or deep-frying. Both are traditional and both are tasty.

- To fry in a skillet: Heat a cast-iron skillet on medium-high heat. Melt a knob of butter in it. Scoop up portions of the cod mixture to fry and flatten it in the pan a little, so you have a thick patty. They will turn golden brown on the bottom. Flip over once so the cakes are golden on both sides. They should cook about 3 minutes total, just to set the egg.

- To deep-fry: Scoop round balls of the codfish mixture and drop into hot 350°F (180°C) oil. If you don't have a thermometer to check, a cube of white bread should turn golden in 60 seconds or less. When the cod balls are golden brown, remove them to drain on newspaper or paper towels.

- Either way, serve piping hot with the tartar sauce alongside.

Notes:

Codfish balls or cakes have been part of New England cooking since the first settlers arrived. The tradition of salting cod goes back over 500 years in Newfoundland. For the American colonies, salt cod was an important food source and a primary export. Salting and drying the fish allows it to keep fresh for a long time, years even! It was perfect to pack onto ships and send to market around the Atlantic. You can find more salted cod recipes from around the world on pages 102, 124, 125, and 126.

Use an equal amount of fresh cod in place of the salted if you wish. My grandmother likes to use fresh cod, mixing up the leftovers from a baked cod and mashed potato supper. This way it is ready to cook up for breakfast or lunch!

BRAZIL

} **CODFISH FRITTERS**

with Green Brazilian Rice

Yield: *24 medium fish balls; 4 servings*

FOR THE FRITTERS:

1 pound (455 g) dried salt cod
2 large russet potatoes, peeled and diced
2 tablespoons (28 ml) olive oil
1 large onion, small chop
3 cloves of garlic, minced
1½ teaspoons salt
⅓ cup (20 g) chopped parsley
½ teaspoon paprika (optional)
2 eggs, separated

FOR THE RICE:

1½ cups (278 g) long-grain white rice
2 tablespoons (28 ml) sunflower or canola oil
1 medium onion, minced
3 cloves of garlic, minced
4 scallions, chopped
3 cups (700 ml) boiling water
½ cup (8 g) chopped cilantro

* Freshen the salt cod the day before. Rinse any dry salt off under running water. Place the fish in a bowl and cover with cool water. Soak this way for 24 hours, changing the water at least 4 times. This extracts most of the salt from the fish.

* Rinse the rice until the water runs clear. Set it aside to dry before making the rice.

* To make the Brazilian-style rice, heat the sunflower oil on medium heat in the pot in which you will make the rice. Add the onion and sweat it for 1 minute. Add the garlic and scallions and cook another minute; don't get any brown color on the onion. Add the dry rice all at once. Stir it around in the hot garlic-infused oil, toasting it, for about 4 minutes. Make sure it does not stick to the bottom of the pan. Add the boiling water, all at once, and stir the rice a few times. Put a good-fitting lid on and simmer on the lowest setting for 20 minutes. When done, fluff the rice with a fork. Serve with the chopped cilantro.

* The cod should now be sufficiently rinsed and soaked and ready to be cooked. Put the small diced potatoes in a pot. Fill it with cool water 2 inches (5 cm) above the potatoes. Bring the water and potatoes to a boil. Boil for 5 minutes, turn it down to a steady simmer, and put in the salt cod. Don't allow the water to boil again or the codfish will be spongy. Cook until the codfish is tender and flaky and the potatoes tender, about 10 minutes. Drain all of it through a colander. Shake off the excess water and transfer it into a bowl.

* Heat the olive oil and the onion in a skillet, over medium heat, making a *refogado*. When the onion is soft and translucent, after 5 minutes, add the garlic. Cook about 2 minutes more. Remove the onion and garlic to the bowl of fish and potatoes. Mash the potatoes, fish, and onions together, removing the big lumps. Mix in the salt, parsley, and paprika, if using.

* Separate the eggs, putting the whites in a mixing bowl and the yolks in another. Mix the yolks into the fish mixture once it has cooled a few minutes. Whisk the whites with a wire whisk to soft peaks. This does not take long to do by hand; it is ideal to stop whisking when the whites cling to the whisk and can hold their shape in a wet, wobbly peak. If it goes beyond this stage, they deflate a bit and look lumpy, which is less ideal.

* Add the whipped egg white to the fish mixture. Mix it in as gently as possible. By whipping the egg whites, we can incorporate air bubbles into the fritters, which will make them lighter and a little puffier.

* To deep-fry the fritters, heat at least 2 inches (5 cm) of oil to 350°F (180°C). Using 2 spoons or an ice cream scoop, drop several balls into the hot oil. When the balls turn golden brown, in about 3 minutes, remove them to drain on newspaper or paper towels. Shower with a sprinkle of salt. Repeat with the remaining batter. Keep warm in a 180°F (82°C) oven until ready to serve with the rice.

Note:

Balls of salted cod, bacalhau, are a hugely popular snack food in Brazil. In Rio, they are served at parties, bars, receptions, and homes and show up in every cookbook. They are clearly beloved and ubiquitous. Try variations of this recipe, adding some bell pepper or tomato to the refogado!

MEXICO

} **FISH ALBONDIGAS**

in Poblano Salsa

Yield: 20 small fish balls; 4 servings

FOR THE ALBONDIGAS:

1½ cups (355 ml) water

1 pound (455 g) fish, such as sea bass, grouper, or tilapia

2 to 3 slices of bread, crusts removed

3 eggs

1 tablespoon (15 ml) lime juice

¾ teaspoon salt

¼ teaspoon black pepper

FOR THE SALSA:

3 poblano chiles, seeds removed, diced

1 tablespoon (15 ml) safflower or canola oil

1 small onion, diced

4 cloves of garlic, minced

½ pound (225 g) ripe tomatoes, diced

½ teaspoon dried Mexican oregano

Salt and pepper, to taste

FOR SERVING:

Cooked rice

- Bring the water to a boil in a medium saucepan. Add a pinch of salt and the fish fillets. Keep the water at a simmer and cook the fish about 5 minutes until it flakes to the touch. Using a slotted spoon, remove the fish to a bowl and save the broth. Flake the fish, removing any bones or skin.

- Dip the bread into the fish broth so it is saturated. Squeeze out extra liquid and add the bread to the flaked fish. Once it is cool, mix in the eggs, lime juice, salt, and pepper. Break up pieces of the bread so everything is in uniform small pieces.

- In a wide pan, sauté the poblano chiles with the oil for about 5 minutes. Add the onions and garlic and cook until soft and tender. Add the diced tomatoes and cook on low so the tomato softens as well. Strain the water the fish was poached in, adding it to the sauce. Depending how juicy your tomatoes were, you may want to add more water. Season the sauce with the oregano, salt, and pepper.

- Bring the sauce to a steady simmer. Form small 1- to 2-inch (2.5 to 5 cm) balls of the fish mixture. Place them into the simmering sauce. Cover the pan and cook on very low heat for 10 minutes. Serve in bowls with rice on the side.

Note:

Albondigas de pescado, or fish meatballs, are popular on the Pacific coast of Mexico. This is a simple dish, and since it uses cooked fish, it is a great thing to make with leftovers of another meal. The salsa is delicious and quick to make; it is best with the freshest tomatoes of summer. If they are out of season, use canned tomatoes.

} # TONGA YAM AND FISH FRITTERS

with Mango Salsa

Yield: *25 large fish balls; 6 to 8 servings*

FOR THE SALSA:

1 ripe mango, peeled and diced
Juice from 2 limes
1 to 2 small hot chiles, seeded and sliced
⅓ cup (55 g) diced red onion
1 handful of cilantro
½ teaspoon salt

FOR THE FRITTERS:

1 cup (235 ml) beer
1 small onion, diced
2 teaspoons salt, divided
1 teaspoon black pepper
1½ pounds (680 g) fresh fish fillets
2½ cups (563 g) cooked yam or sweet potatoes
⅓ cup (80 ml) coconut milk
½ cup (63 g) all-purpose flour, on a plate
1 to 2 cups (235 to 475 ml) oil for frying

* To make the salsa, cut everything small and toss it all into a bowl. Cover and let sit while the fritters are being made so the flavors in the salsa can meld. This can be done up to 3 days ahead. If the fritters will be eaten while standing up and you want a sauce thin enough to dip them in, send the salsa through the blender or food processor.

* In a small saucepan, heat the beer, onion, and half the salt and pepper. With the beer at a simmer, add the fish and cook it for 5 minutes at most, so that it flakes when touched with a spoon. Strain the fish and onion and place in a mixing bowl.

* To the same bowl as the fish, add the cooked yam, coconut milk, and remaining salt and pepper. Mix the ingredients with a wooden spoon until combined and close to fluffy.

* Roll portions of the mixture into 2-inch-wide (5 cm) balls. Coat entirely in flour.

* Heat a few inches of oil (7.5 to 10 cm) for frying, in a pan or wok, to 350°F (180°C). Deep-fry the fish fritters, turning once or twice in the oil so they turn golden brown all over. They should cook in only 2 to 3 minutes. Remove with a slotted spoon and drain on newspaper or paper towels.

* Serve hot with the mango salsa or simply with lemon. They are a tasty snack or appetizer, sure to disappear quickly.

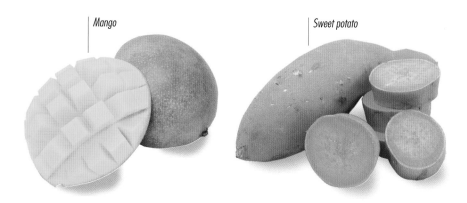

Mango

Sweet potato

AUSTRALIA

QUICK POTATO, CORN, AND TUNA FISH BALLS

Yield: 14 large fish balls; 3 to 4 servings

1 cup (210 g) potato, cooked and mashed, or ½ pound (225 g) raw)

2 cans (5 ounces, or 140 g each) tuna in water

½ cup (77 g) corn kernels (fresh or frozen, defrosted)

½ cup (50 g) scallions, sliced (about 6)

1 tablespoon (15 ml) lemon juice

½ teaspoon sea salt

¼ teaspoon black pepper

Chili sauce, to taste

2 eggs, divided

Cornmeal

* Leftover mashed or baked potatoes make this recipe come together very quickly. If cooking the potatoes specifically, peel and roughly dice ½ pound (225 g) of potatoes. Place in a saucepan, cover with cold water, and add a large pinch of salt. Boil the potatoes until fork tender and drain.

* In a large mixing bowl, mash the potatoes with a fork until broken up into small pieces. Drain the tuna well. Add the tuna, corn, scallions, lemon juice, sea salt, pepper, and chili sauce to the potato. Mix all together with a fork, taste the mixture to test for enough salt and spice, and adjust as necessary. Add 1 egg and mix in well.

* Crack 1 egg into a small bowl and beat well. Spread the cornmeal into another shallow bowl. Form the mixture into 2-inch (5 cm) balls. Dredge each ball first in egg, then cornmeal. Place on a foil-lined baking tray.

* Bake in a 400°F (200°C, or gas mark 6) preheated oven for 20 minutes. The cornmeal crust should be golden, toasted, and crispy, with some dark spots. Serve while hot; these are best eaten when freshly made.

Tip:

Serve these tuna fish balls with slices of avocado, scallions, and mayonnaise. Or make smaller balls and serve as warm appetizers.

GINGER AND SCALLION NAMERO MACKEREL BALLS

Yield: *30 medium fish balls; 5 servings*

FOR THE MACKEREL BALLS:

5 whole mackerel, filleted into 10 fillets
3 to 4 scallions, chopped small
¾ teaspoon salt
1 to 2 tablespoons (16 to 32 g) miso paste
1 tablespoon (8 g) grated fresh ginger
Canola or safflower oil, for frying

FOR SERVING:

Cooked short-grained sticky rice

* Place the mackerel fillets onto a cutting board; plastic is best for cleaning. Using a large chopping knife, turn the fillets into smaller pieces. Pile them up and chop over them again and again. Slide under the fish pile with the knife occasionally and flip the pile over. Once it is quite minced, use the blunt back side of the knife to work over the fish a few times. You are looking for a fine, evenly minced pile of fish, not a purée. This is one time where chopping by hand does seem to make a big difference in texture over using a food processor, but it can be used in a pinch. Be supercareful to not overprocess it.

* Mix in the scallions, salt, miso paste, and grated ginger. You can use the same knife to mix them in.

* Heat 2 inches (5 cm) of oil in a wok, or a small pan with high sides, to 350°F (180°C) or when a test piece bubbles violently immediately after contact with the oil. Form small ping-pong ball–size balls of the minced fish. Drop one in the oil, flip over once golden brown on the bottom, and remove to drain on paper towels. Taste this one to ensure the fish balls don't need more salt or miso. Once satisfied, continue to fry the remaining fish, as many portions are comfortably fit in your frying oil without crowding. Drain them well on paper and keep warm in a 180°F (82°C) oven until serving with short-grained sticky rice.

Note:

Namero is traditionally served raw in Japan, like sushi. Occasionally, it is poached in soup. Try any of the variations. If you do try it raw, be sure your fish is the freshest sushi grade.

} POACHED SALMON BALLS

Yield: *25 small fish balls; 4 servings*

FOR THE SAUCE:

½ cup (70 g) diced, peeled cucumber
1 cup (230 g) sour cream
2 to 3 tablespoons (8 to 12 g) chopped fresh dill
½ teaspoon salt
Black pepper, to taste

FOR THE SALMON BALLS:

1 pound (455 g) salmon, skin and bones removed
½ cup (120 ml) whole milk
1 egg
1 teaspoon salt
½ teaspoon black pepper
1 tablespoon (12 g) potato starch or (8 g)
*   cornstarch*

FOR SERVING:

Pickled beets
Lemon
Horseradish

* To make the sauce, simply mix the peeled and diced cucumber with the sour cream, dill, salt, and pepper to taste. Keep cool until ready to eat.

* Cut the salmon into chunks to fit into a food processor. Purée the fish until it becomes a fine paste. Add the milk and the remaining ingredients. Purée about 10 seconds or as long as necessary to make the mixture very smooth.

* Heat a large pot of salted water on the stove, bringing it just to a light simmer. With a spoon, scoop up a bite-size portion of the salmon. You can form egg shapes using 2 spoons. Or, to form balls, use the spoon and the palm of your other hand. Wet your hand with cold water and draw the spoon across your cupped palm, coaxing the salmon into a round shape. As each is finished, drop it into the water. They will sink at first and float at the top when halfway cooked. Allow them to cook an extra minute or two on the surface to cook through.

* With a slotted spoon, remove the poached salmon to a warm plate. Cover with the sauce and serve warm or at room temperature. If you have leftovers, they are even good chilled, just as regular poached salmon is.

* Serve with pickled beets, lemon, or horseradish.

Note:

Scandinavian-style poached salmon fillets with cucumber cream sauce is a delicate dish popular at weddings and luncheons. By turning them into balls, the result is an even lighter, more unexpected dish, which adults and children are sure to love. There is an abundance of farm-raised salmon these days, and the price is reasonable. Wild salmon remains superior in all other counts, including flavor, nutrition, and color.

ITALY

}

SICILIAN TUNA BALLS

with Roasted Tomatoes

Yield: *25 medium fish balls; 4 to 5 servings*

FOR THE TOMATOES:

9 fresh plum tomatoes

4 tablespoons (60 ml) good olive oil

Salt and fresh ground black pepper

6 cloves of garlic

Thyme or oregano

FOR THE TUNA BALLS:

2 slices of stale bread, crusts removed

⅓ cup (80 ml) milk

1 pound (455 g) fresh tuna

3 tablespoons (12 g) finely chopped parsley

2 tablespoons (12 g) finely chopped fresh mint

Zest of 1 lemon

¼ cup (36 g) pine nuts

2 tablespoons (10 g) grated cheese, Pecorino or Parmesan

1 egg

Salt and black pepper

All-purpose flour for dredging

Olive oil for cooking

FOR SERVING:

Fresh salad

Lemon wedges

- Preheat the oven to 325°F (170°C, or gas mark 3). Cut the tomatoes in half and choose a baking dish that will accommodate all of them in a single layer. Drizzle the olive oil all over the pan and the tomatoes, tossing them to coat. Arrange the tomatoes cut side down. Sprinkle with salt, pepper, and the garlic and herb. Roast in the oven for 40 minutes. Remove the tray, turn the tomatoes over, and return to the oven. Increase the heat to 400°F (200°C, or gas mark 6). Roast for about 20 more minutes.

- Soak the crustless bread in the milk for 5 minutes until soft.

- Cut the tuna into 2-inch (5 cm) pieces. Place the tuna and parsley, mint, lemon zest, pine nuts, cheese, egg, salt, and pepper into the food processor. Remove the bread from the milk and add the bread as well. Pulse to combine and chop the tuna into smaller pieces, not a pulp. This can be accomplished with a knife and cutting board as well.

- Heat ½ inch (1.3 cm) of olive oil in a skillet for frying. When it is hot enough, a test piece should sizzle straight away. Prevent the oil from getting so hot that it smokes. Scoop up portions of the tuna mixture to make small balls about 1½ inches (3.8 cm) across. Roll each ball in flour before adding to the hot oil. Fill the pan without crowding it; it may take a few batches to finish the frying. Cook them for about 7 minutes until browned on the outside and just cooked through. Raw tuna is perfectly lovely to eat, but be sure your tuna is sushi grade and your guests are into it before you decide to undercook them. Remove the tuna balls to paper towels or newspaper to drain. Keep warm in the oven until serving.

- Serve the tuna balls with a few roasted tomatoes, a fresh salad, and lemon wedges.

Note:

To substitute the tuna, don't try to use the canned variety, but any fresh dark, meaty fish will do: amberjack, bluefish, mackerel, king mackerel, or wahoo are some options.

USA

LOBSTER AND GRITS CROQUETTES
with Garlic Leafy Greens

Yield: *30 large fish balls; 6 to 8 servings*

FOR THE GRITS:

4½ cups (1 L) water

1½ teaspoons salt

1 cup (140 g) hominy grits

1 cup (225 g) cooked chopped lobster, shrimp, or crawfish meat

½ cup (60 g) grated Cheddar cheese

¼ teaspoon black pepper

Pinch of dry mustard

FOR COOKING:

All-purpose flour for dredging

1 egg, beaten

Fine crushed cracker or bread crumbs

Oil for frying, like peanut or safflower

FOR THE GREENS:

1 pound (455 g) leafy greens (collard, kale, or chard)

2 tablespoons (28 ml) olive oil

5 cloves of garlic, minced

Salt and black pepper

* Bring the water and salt to a vigorous boil in your most heavy-bottomed 3-quart (2.8 L) saucepan. I find an enameled cast-iron one does the job best. With a wire whisk in one hand continuously stirring the boiling water, slowly sprinkle in the grits. Adding the grits in a slow stream while whisking prevents clumps from forming. When all the grits are added, reduce the heat to low and continue stirring until the heat lessens and only the occasional bubble breaks at the surface. Cook for 30 to 40 minutes on the lowest setting. Stir occasionally to check the bottom isn't sticking or burning, a common problem in pans that are too thin. The grits will thicken within the first several minutes of cooking, but it takes more time to cook the grain through, unless you use quick-cook grits, which are fast but not as tasty as the old-fashioned slow-cook ones.

* Meanwhile, chop the lobster or shrimp into bite-size morsels, small enough to mix into the croquettes but large enough they will be appreciated as shellfish. This is a nice way to use up leftover boiled lobster or shrimp cocktail from parties.

* To cook the greens, bring a pot of water to a boil. Wash and chop the greens into pieces, removing the toughest stems. Simmer the greens for 5 minutes in the water. This extracts much of the bitter taste. Drain in a colander in the sink and let the greens drip dry for a moment. In the same pot, to lessen the washing up, sauté the olive oil and garlic for 1 to 2 minutes, just so it begins to turn golden. Add the greens to the garlic and sauté about 5 minutes until tender. Season with salt and pepper to taste.

* Take the finished grits off the heat and stir in the cheese. If you wait till the grits cool, they set up too hard to mix in the cheese. Fold in the lobster pieces, black pepper, and mustard. Set aside to cool.

* Heat the frying oil to 350°F (180°C). Set up shallow bowls for dredging: one bowl with flour, a second bowl with the well-beaten egg, and a third bowl with the cracker crumbs. Shape the cool, but not cold, grits into balls, each the size of an egg. Right before frying each one, roll the ball in the flour and shake off any excess. Dip in the egg and then finally in the cracker crumbs. Lower into the hot oil, cooking until golden brown, flipping over at least once. Remove to drain on paper towels. Continue until all the grit balls are fried. Serve at once, hot, melty, and crunchy with the luscious and flavorful greens.

4

Veggie Balls

Vegetables were probably the first food made into balls, ever since early human beings made the first grain porridges and mashed root vegetables. In many parts of Africa today, this tradition continues as foofoo, balls of starchy vegetables eaten with stew, and in the round fritters that are made the next day from leftovers. Every culture has their own versions and flavors to transform their potatoes, beans, tofu, lentils, and plantains.

Sometimes vegetable balls are disguised to seem like meat, as a replacement when meat is scarce or for those who abstain. Other times the vegetable is celebrated. Making it into a ball elevates the plain vegetable to something special. Both adults and children who claim to dislike vegetables, tofu, or lentils will find balls of them charming and irresistible: balls of goodness just waiting to be bitten into.

JAPAN

} **PUFFY FRIED TOFU BALLS**

Agedashi Tofu

Yield: *10–12 large veggieballs; 5 servings*

1 block firm tofu, 14 ounces (390 g)
2 cups (475 ml) water
4 tablespoons (60 ml) soy sauce
3 tablespoons (45 ml) mirin
1 tablespoon (0.8 g) dried bonito flakes
1 piece kombu, 2 inches (5 cm)
¾ teaspoon salt
1 teaspoon grated fresh ginger
¼ cup (48 g) potato starch or (32 g) cornstarch
¼ cup (25 g) scallions, for serving

* Drain excess water from the tofu on cloth or paper towels or with a weight on top, such as a cutting board. This takes about 15 minutes.

* Mix the water, soy sauce, mirin, bonito flakes, and kombu seaweed in a small saucepan. Simmer for 5 minutes. Remove from the heat.

* With a potato masher or muddler, crush the tofu in a mixing bowl for about 1 minute. It will resemble cottage cheese in texture when it is ready. Add the salt and grated fresh ginger into the tofu. Mix to combine.

* Place the starch into a dish for dredging. Form golf ball–size portions of tofu into balls by compressing, not rolling, in the palm of your hand. Roll each ball into the starch to coat it all over. Set aside to await frying.

* Heat about 2 inches (5 cm) of oil to deep-fry the tofu balls. An easy way to use less oil is to fry in a wok; you will only be able to fry 2, maybe 3 balls at a time, but it requires far less oil. Heat the oil until very hot, 300°F (150°C); a piece of scallion top dunked into the hot oil should sizzle wildly right away.

* Fry a few balls at a time, turning to make all sides golden. They are done when slightly puffed with pale golden outsides. If they begin to crack or split, they are just past done. Remove to a paper towel to drain; do not cover. Serve straight away, while warm, with the scallions, which are very important for the flavor and texture balance. Spoon the dashi broth into bowls immediately before eating because the tofu balls quickly absorb the liquid and the texture will change.

Note:

These will make you feel as if you are in your favorite Japanese restaurant: elegant, simple, and perfectly paired. A delicate side dish or appetizer, it's worth the hassle of frying. These do not reheat well, except in a soup, but they will all be eaten up, so no worries.

ECUADOR

GREEN PLANTAIN AND CHEESE BALLS

Bolón de Verde

Yield: *12–15 large veggieballs; 3 to 4 servings*

4 green plantains

4 to 5 tablespoons (55 to 70 g) lard or butter

1 teaspoon ground cumin

2 teaspoons chili powder

1 teaspoon salt

1 cup (115 g) grated Asadero or provolone cheese

2 tablespoons (28 ml) sunflower or canola oil

- Peel the plantains by first cutting off the top and bottom and running a knife down the length of opposite sides. Use the knife to pry the skin off the fruit. The greener they are, the more difficult to pry the peel off. With some practice, it will become simple. If there are any spots where the peel is stuck, just cut it off with the knife. Be warned, plantain peel can stain your cutting boards or hands sort of black. Work quickly with the peels, throw them directly into the trash, and you should not have a problem.

- Cut the plantains into 1-inch (2.5 cm) slices. Melt the butter over medium heat in a skillet and add the plantain chunks. Cook slowly for nearly 40 minutes. Turn every 10 minutes or so. They will turn golden but shouldn't be very crispy.

- Transfer the plantains to a big bowl. Add the cumin, chili powder, and salt. While hot, mash the plantains with a muddler or a potato masher. When they have been mashed into a chunky paste, they are ready. If it is still too hot to handle, allow it to cool a bit longer.

- Form balls of plantain that are 2 to 3 (5 to 7.5 cm) inches wide: bigger than golf balls and smaller than tennis balls. Make a deep hole in the middle of each ball, take some cheese, press it into the hole, and cover the filling by pressing the plantain back into the shape of a ball. Repeat with all the balls.

- Heat the oil in the same skillet over high heat. Fry the plantain balls until golden and crispy on the outsides. Serve immediately to people who are about to be very happy.

Plantain

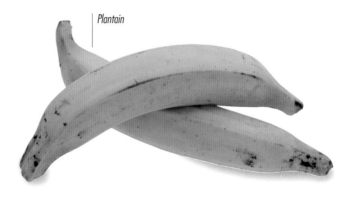

INDIA

GINGER AND CHILE LENTIL FRITTERS

Yield: *15 small veggieballs; 3 to 5 servings*

5 ounces (140 g) yellow split lentils (channa dhal)
5 ounces (140 g) split mung beans (mung dhal)
1½ inches (3.8 cm) ginger, sliced
2 to 4 dried small red chiles
Zest of half a lime
Pinch of salt
1 big red onion, quartered
Sunflower oil, for frying

- Combine the lentils and beans in a bowl. Wash them, cover with cold water, and pour most of it out. Cover with water again and pour most of it out. Repeat until the water is clear. Cover with water one last time and set aside to soak for 2 to 4 hours.

- Drain the lentils in a colander.

- Place the lentils, ginger, chiles, lime zest, and salt into a food processor. Blend for about 30 seconds, looking for a coarse paste. Add the onion and pulse to chop the onion into fine pieces. The mixture should be coarse but all small pieces.

- Scoop the lentil mixture into about 15 small balls only about 1 inch (2.5 cm) wide.

- Heat 1½ inches (3.8 cm) of oil for deep-frying to 350°F (180°C) in a pot with high sides or in a wok. A test piece should sizzle like crazy on immediate contact with the hot oil. Fry in batches to not crowd the surface of the oil. The balls should cook for about 5 minutes. Turn them over a few times during cooking so they turn an even brown. Remove to paper towels to drain.

- The crispy fritters can be served with tea or coffee as a midafternoon snack. Or make a double or triple batch and serve as munchies at a cocktail party.

Note:

These lentil fritters are eaten as a snack during Southern Indian Pongal festivities, a January harvest festival. There are 4 days of celebrations honoring nature, the rain, and sun, with bonfires, family visits, and special dishes. Cows and bulls are celebrated and have perhaps the best day of their year, decked out in flowers and colorful paints and given baths in the river and fed sweets.

MOROCCO

WALNUT, ZA'ATAR, AND EGGPLANT KUFTEH

Yield: *14 medium veggieballs; 4 servings*

1 russet potato
1 large Italian eggplant (1½ cups [149 g] puréed)
½ cup (60 g) finely chopped walnuts
½ cup (60 g) bread crumbs
¼ cup (15 g) chopped parsley
⅓ teaspoon black pepper
½ teaspoon salt
1 egg
1 teaspoon ground cumin
½ teaspoon ground coriander
3 tablespoons (45 ml) olive oil
2 tablespoons (8 g) za'atar (See Tip.)
2 tablespoons (14 g) bread crumbs
Vegetable oil, for cooking

- Wrap the potato in aluminum foil. Place the potato and the whole eggplant on a baking tray. Roast in a 350°F (180°C, or gas mark 4) oven until the eggplant is soft and collapses when poked, about 45 minutes to 1 hour.

- Cut the top off the eggplant and slice it in half. Scoop out the insides of the potato and the eggplant, discarding the skins. Purée the eggplant and the potato in the food processor for 1 to 2 minutes. It should be a fairly smooth paste and about 2 cups (455 g) in total.

- Add the walnuts, bread crumbs, parsley, pepper, salt, egg, cumin, coriander, and olive oil. Mix well to incorporate it all.

- Mix the za'atar and bread crumbs together in a bowl.

- Using 2 soup spoons, form an egg-shaped portion of the eggplant mixture. Drop it into the za'atar crumbs. Shake the bowl so it rolls around to be coated with the crumbs. Lift out gently and line up to cook. Repeat with all the eggplant mixture. It will be soft but sets up once cooked.

- Preheat the oven to 350°F (180°C, or gas mark 4). In a heavy-bottomed skillet, heat enough vegetable oil to coat the bottom. Once it is shimmering hot, add about half of the kufteh, not crowding the pan. As the bottoms turn golden brown, roll each kufteh over gently with a spoon. Repeat until all sides are toasted, about 4 minutes. Remove to a baking tray and continue frying the remaining kufteh. Place all of the kufteh into the oven for another 10 to 15 minutes of cooking; this is what really firms up the eggplant. They are done when they are firm, and they may begin to crack a bit. You can skip the frying step and bake them for 30 minutes, but the crust is more luscious if fried first.

- These reheat well the following day; warm them in a skillet to return some of the crunch.

Tip:

Za'atar is a multipurpose spice blend available at Middle Eastern and well-stocked supermarkets. Blends vary widely in taste and color, from green to red. The classic Jordanian blend consists of sumac, sesame seeds, salt, and lots of a bright green herb named Za'atar, which tastes like a mix between oregano and thyme. It is worth picking up some of this spice blend or making it yourself because it is good on everything!

SPAIN } # TAPAS CHICKPEA BALLS

Yield: *24 small veggieballs; 4 to 6 servings*

1 can (15 ounces, or 425 g) chickpeas
3 cloves of garlic
¼ cup (30 g) bread crumbs
¾ teaspoon ground cumin
¼ teaspoon ground coriander
¼ teaspoon paprika
¼ teaspoon ground cinnamon
¼ teaspoon allspice
1 egg
4 tablespoons (60 ml) olive oil
Zest from 1 lemon
½ teaspoon salt
Olive oil, for cooking

- Drain and rinse the chickpeas. Place in the bowl of a food processor with the garlic cloves and bread crumbs. Pulse the chickpeas for about 10 seconds until they are crumbly and coarsely chopped. Add in the spices, egg, oil, lemon zest, and salt. Pulse until the mixture is mostly smooth. Some larger pieces of chickpea provide nice texture. (A potato masher may be substituted for the food processor.)

- Using 2 spoons or a small scoop, form 1-inch (2.5 cm) balls of the chickpea mixture. It is quite soft. Place the balls on a waxed paper–lined tray. Chill the balls in the fridge for 30 minutes or in the freezer for 15 minutes. Chilling firms up the balls and makes the outside a little bit dryer to make for better cooking results.

- These can be baked or pan-fried, with equally delicious but somewhat different results. The pan-fry method is more traditional to Spanish cooking.

- To pan-fry, pour several glugs of olive oil in a skillet, heated on high. When the oil is hot, place the chilled chickpea balls in the oil. Cook in batches if necessary to not crowd the pan. After a golden brown crust forms on the base, turn them with a spoon. Fry as many sides as possible before removing to drain on a paper towel.

- To bake, preheat the oven to 350°F (180°C, or gas mark 4). Arrange the balls on a parchment paper–lined pan. Bake for 20 to 25 minutes. The base will be golden brown, the crust dry, and some of the balls may crack. The inside will still be creamy.

- Serve while hot.

MIDDLE EAST

RED LENTIL AND BULGUR KUFTEH

in Lettuce Leaves

Yield: 20 medium veggieballs; 5 servings

FOR THE KUFTEH:

1 teaspoon cumin seeds
½ cup (96 g) red lentils
2 cups (475 ml) water
½ cup (70 g) bulgur wheat
½ teaspoon salt, divided
3 tablespoons (45 ml) extra virgin olive oil, divided
1 medium onion, finely minced
1 handful of flat-leaf parsley, finely chopped
¼ teaspoon Aleppo pepper (optional)

FOR SERVING:

About 20 lettuce leaves
Chopped parsley
Lemon slices

- Toast the cumin seed in a dry pan on high heat. When the cumin becomes fragrant and the seeds darken a little, remove the seeds to a mortar and pestle or spice grinder. Grind the cumin seeds. Both toasting and grinding the cumin seeds act to increase the flavor.

- Combine the lentils and water in a medium saucepan, bring to a boil, skim off any foam, reduce the heat, and simmer 30 minutes. Not all of the water will be absorbed.

- Add the bulgur and ¼ teaspoon salt into the pot with the lentils. Stir together and then cover and let sit for 30 minutes until the bulgur is tender and all the liquid is absorbed.

- Heat 2 tablespoons (28 ml) of olive oil over medium heat. Add the onion and the remaining salt. Cook slowly for 10 to 15 minutes until transparent and tender. Stir often. Add the ground cumin and stir together for about 30 seconds. Then stir into the lentils and bulgur.

- Using a wooden spoon or spatula, beat the lentil mixture in the bowl for 3 to 5 minutes. This makes the mixture creamy. If it seems dry and crumbly, add a tablespoon (15 ml) of water at a time. Stir in the remaining tablespoon (15 ml) of olive oil, parsley, and Aleppo pepper. Taste and adjust the seasonings.

- Using 2 soup spoons, form the lentil mixture into quenelles (football shapes). Or moisten your hands and shape the mixture into small, lime-size balls. Moisten your hands again whenever the mixture begins to stick. Place on lettuce leaves arranged on a platter. Garnish with parsley and lemon slices.

- Serve cold or at room temperature. Kufteh are eaten by hand, wrapped in a lettuce leaf.

Red lentils

JAPAN

}

ONIGIRI RICE BALLS
with Smoked Salmon and Sesame Seeds

Yield: *8 large veggieballs; 4 servings*

FOR THE RICE:

2 cups (400 g) short-grain Japanese "sushi rice"
2¼ cups (535 ml) water

TO FORM THE ONIGIRI:

6 ounces (170 g) smoked salmon
2 tablespoons (16 g) toasted sesame seeds
Water
Salt
2 sheets nori, cut into 2-inch-wide (5 cm) strips

Sesame seeds

- To make the rice, use a heavy-bottomed pot with a tight-fitting lid. Measure the rice into the pot, put it in the sink, and cover it with water. Mix it around with your hand; the water will turn milky white. Dump out most of the cloudy water. Cover it with water again, swish, and dump it out. Do this several more times until the water is almost clear. Now drain the rice in a sieve for 15 minutes. Now, finally, put the rice and 2¼ cups water (535 ml) into the pot or rice cooker. On the stove, bring the pot to a boil, boil for 3 minutes, turn the heat to low heat, and cover for 15 minutes. Then turn off the heat, remove the lid, and drape a clean tea towel over the top. This absorbs extra moisture while letting the rice continue to cook.

- Heat a nonstick pan over medium heat. Cook the slices of salmon for about 30 seconds on both sides, until just opaque. Put into a bowl; the salmon should now be easy to flake with a fork into small bits. Combine the sesame seeds, salmon, and the rice all together. Mix well.

- Onigiri are formed while the rice is hot, so it sticks together. You can form it with your hands, wetted in cool water, but the hot rice can be uncomfortable. Here is an easy way: gather some sturdy plastic wrap and a small bowl the size you desire the rice balls to be; a teacup works well. Drape a piece of plastic wrap inside the teacup. Drip a little bit of water on the plastic wrap and

dump out any puddle of water. Sprinkle a bit of salt on the plastic wrap also; this flavors the outside of the rice so it is very savory. Scoop the rice mixture into the plastic-wrapped cup, just to the top. Gather the ends of the plastic wrap together. Lift the bunch out of the teacup. Twist the plastic together at the top while squeezing it into a ball. Let any extra air out, so it can be a very compact sphere. Squeeze it well in your hands so that the rice ball is one unit.

- To eat or serve, unwrap and discard the plastic. Take a strip of nori and wrap it around the rice ball. This adds flavor and creates a charming way to hold the onigiri while eating it.

- If you want to eat the balls later, you can keep them in the plastic wrapping to stay fresh. They travel well; bring them to lunch or out on a picnic! If you do, just pack some strips of nori next to them, because the nori will lose its crispy quality soon after being wrapped on the rice, although it does remain tasty.

Note:

Onigiri is a basic comfort food. It is simply a ball or triangle of salty rice wrapped in seaweed, sometimes with a filling. In Japan, they are sold at every market and convenience store, even in vending machines. People have them as a snack, on hikes, in cars, and in bento box lunches; they are portable and comforting and travel everywhere. There are many gadgets designed to make onigiri in the shape of cute animals, and it is such a beloved food there are anime characters and little plastic toys shaped like onigiri.

ITALY

} # NEXT DAY BAKED ARANCINI

Yield: *16 large veggieballs; 4 servings*

FOR THE ARANCINI:

½ cup (63 g) all-purpose flour
1 cup (50 g) panko or (115 g) bread crumbs
1 egg
3 cups (495 g) cold risotto, or plain rice leftovers
5 ounces (140 g) mozzarella cheese
Olive oil spray

SERVING SUGGESTIONS:

Green salad
Marinara sauce

* Preheat the oven to 425°F (220°C, or gas mark 7). Prepare a baking tray by spraying it with oil or lining it with parchment paper. Put the flour into a shallow dish and the panko into another dish. Crack the egg in a bowl and beat it well.

* Cold risotto sticks together in a helpful way. Roll the cold risotto into 2-inch-wide (5 cm) balls. An ice cream scoop works well for this. Use your finger to press a chunk of mozzarella cheese into the center of each ball. Roll to return to a ball shape. Coat each ball in flour, then egg, finally rolling in the panko to coat. Place the balls onto the baking tray with at least 2 inches (5 cm) of space between each one so they brown well. For extra-crispy crust, use olive oil spray and mist the top and sides of the arancini.

* Bake for 25 minutes until crispy, golden, and hot throughout. Green salad is a good companion for arancini or a pool of tomato marinara sauce.

Note:

Arancini are made from leftover risotto, which doesn't heat up to its same creamy glory on the second day but makes phenomenal creamy arancini. You can use regular cooked rice, although it is just a little more difficult to get to stick together.

RUSSIA

} POTATO BALL AND MILK SOUP

Yield: *24 small veggieballs; 2 servings*

FOR THE POTATO DUMPLINGS:

¾ pound (340 g) raw potatoes, or 1½ cups
   (315 g) cooked, cold, mashed
2½ tablespoons (30 g) potato starch
1½ tablespoons (23 ml) milk
½ teaspoon salt
1 egg

FOR THE SOUP:

2 cups (475 ml) milk, or to cover dumplings
Salt and black pepper, to taste
Pinch of allspice

* Peel and roughly dice ¾ pound (340 g) of potatoes. Place in a saucepan, cover with cold water, and add a large pinch of salt. Boil the potatoes until fork tender and drain.

* Leftover mashed or baked potatoes make this recipe come together very quickly. If making with leftover potatoes, adjust the recipe if the leftovers already have milk or salt added.

* In a large mixing bowl, mash the potatoes with a fork until broken up into small pieces. Add the potato starch, milk, salt, and egg. Mix it up well with a fork until uniform.

* Pour the milk into a wide saucepan on low heat. Add a pinch of salt and pepper and a tiny pinch of allspice. Roll the potato dough into tiny 1-inch (2.5 cm) balls and place directly into the milk, even if it is not yet warm. Repeat until all the dough is in the milk. Little bubbles around the side of the pan are good; however, do not allow the milk to come to a simmer or a boil! Potato balls should be submerged ¾ of the way, so add more milk if necessary. Cook the dumplings and milk on the lowest setting for 20 to 30 minutes. Serve with fresh ground pepper.

Note:

This soup is an old-fashioned comfort food from the area around western Russia and Germany. It is wonderfully simple and ideal on a cold winter day, and children tend to love it. Potato starch can be substituted with potato flour, arrowroot powder, or cornstarch.

} VEGETARIAN MATZO BALL SOUP

Yield: *12 large veggieballs; 6 servings*

FOR THE MATZO BALLS:

2 eggs

2 tablespoons (28 ml) grapeseed oil

2 tablespoons (28 ml) seltzer water

½ cup (58 g) matzo meal (See Tip.)

½ teaspoon kosher salt

¼ teaspoon black pepper

¼ teaspoon onion powder

2 teaspoons chopped fresh dill

3 quarts (2.8 L) water

1 pinch of saffron

FOR THE SOUP:

1 tablespoon (15 ml) olive oil

3 carrots, thinly sliced

2 to 3 quarts (1.9 to 2.8 L) good-quality vegetable stock

Salt and pepper, to taste

Dill fronds, for serving

* Use a fork to whisk the eggs, oil, and seltzer water together. Add the matzo meal, salt, pepper, onion powder, and dill. Stir into a thick batter. Place in the fridge to rest for 30 minutes.

* Bring the water to a simmer with a pinch of salt and a pinch of saffron threads. The saffron makes the balls a beautiful yellow and imparts a mysterious flavor that does a good job of replacing the missing chicken.

* Roll the matzo ball dough into walnut-size balls. They expand a lot while cooking. The dough can be very sticky; wet your hands frequently to make neat balls. Put all the balls into the simmering water. Once they are all in, bring the heat back to a steady simmer, cover the pot, and let them cook for 30 minutes to cook through. Keep them in the hot water if you are eating within the hour. If you want to save them for later, remove with a slotted spoon and keep covered in the fridge. They will turn soggy if kept in the water too long.

* In a large soup pot, heat the olive oil and carrot on medium-low heat. It is not necessary to brown the carrot, but the olive oil gives it a good flavor. Add the vegetable stock and bring to a boil. Add salt and pepper to season the soup well.

* Serve by placing 2 warm matzo balls into a soup bowl and covering with vegetable broth, carrots, and a sprig of dill.

Tip:

If you cannot find the matzo meal, simply put a few matzo crackers into the food processor and turn it on for a minute or two. You want really fine crumbs, almost matzo dust.

} # FALAFEL

with Mint Yogurt Sauce

Yield: *20 large veggieballs; 4 to 5 servings*

FOR THE FALAFEL:

1¼ cups (250 g) dried chickpeas
1 small yellow onion, quartered
2 gloves of garlic, smashed
3 tablespoons (12 g) chopped parsley
1 teaspoon salt
¼ teaspoon cayenne pepper
¾ teaspoon ground coriander
¼ teaspoon cardamom
¾ teaspoon ground cumin
½ teaspoon baking powder
1½ tablespoons (12 g) all-purpose flour
3 tablespoons (45 ml) cold water
3 to 4 cups (700 to 950 ml) sunflower or
  peanut oil for deep-frying

FOR THE MINT YOGURT SAUCE:

2 cups (460 g) plain goat or cow yogurt
1 tablespoon (2 g) dried mint
2½ tablespoons (15 g) fresh chopped mint
2 tablespoons (28 ml) fresh lemon juice
½ teaspoon salt
Fresh ground black pepper

FOR SERVING:

Pita bread
Hummus
Fresh salad

- To make falafel, soak the dried chickpeas in water for 24 hours.

- Drain and rinse the rehydrated chickpeas. Combine with the onion, garlic, parsley, and salt. Chop this mixture to bits using a food processor or meat grinder. Work in batches to get a good result. Run each batch in the food processor for 30 to 40 seconds until they are very finely chopped, but not puréed or pasty. With it all in one large bowl now, add the spices and baking powder, flour, and water. Mix by hand, kneading until it is more smooth and holds together when coaxed into a ball.

- Ideally, let the mixture rest in the fridge 1 hour before frying. Falafel mixture can be made up to this step and kept 1 day well covered in the fridge.

- Heat 2 to 3 inches (5 to 7.5 cm) of oil in a heavy pot with tall sides suitable for deep-frying. The oil should be 350°F (180°C). Scoop portions of the falafel mixture to make balls 1½ to 2 inches (3.8 to 5 cm) wide, about 1 ounce (28 g) each. An ice cream scoop or spoon can help, but hands do the best job of gently compressing and rounding the falafel. Lower each one into the hot oil as it is formed. Turn occasionally in the oil till a nutty brown on all sides, 3 to 5 minutes. Don't crowd the pan or the oil will drop in temperature. Remove with a slotted spoon and drain on plenty of paper towels or newspapers.

- To make the mint yogurt sauce, toss the yogurt, dried and fresh mints, lemon juice, salt, and pepper into a jar with a tight-fitting lid. Screw the lid on tightly and shake vigorously. This is an easy way to mix up a sauce, with no utensils to wash! A bowl and a spoon work perfectly well also.

- Serve warm with mint yogurt sauce, pitas, hummus, and fresh salad.

Fresh mint

Note:

It is important to soak the dried chickpeas for an entire day to ensure they are well hydrated. If not properly soaked, they will not cook all the way. The flavor and texture are incredible compared to the canned variety.

USA

QUINOA ZUCCHINI AND SWEET POTATO BALLS

Yield: *24 large veggieballs; 6 servings*

¾ cup (139 g) dry quinoa

1½ cups (355 ml) water

6 ounces (170 g) sweet potato or yam, peeled and diced

1 cup (120 g) zucchini, grated and squeezed

1 tablespoon (4 g) chopped parsley

¾ teaspoon dried sage

½ teaspoon black pepper

1 teaspoon salt

1 tablespoon (3 g) chives or (6 g) scallions

¼ teaspoon chili powder

1 tablespoon (15 ml) olive oil

1 tablespoon (15 ml) lemon juice

- Rinse the quinoa in a fine strainer. Bring the water, quinoa, and sweet potato to a boil; turn the heat to low and cover the pot for 25 minutes. Take off the heat, leave the lid on, and rest 5 minutes before fluffing with a fork.

- While the quinoa is cooking, shred and wring out the zucchini. Too much moisture will make the balls mushy. Mix the zucchini, parsley, sage, pepper, salt, chives, chili powder, olive oil, and lemon juice in a large bowl. Add the total 2 cups (370 g) of fluffed quinoa and sweet potato to the bowl. Mix it all very well, mashing the sweet potato in the process.

- Preheat the oven to 350°F (180°C, or gas mark 4). Use an ice cream scoop or a spoon to help shape the mixture into 1½ to 2 inch (3.8 to 5 cm) balls. Place them on parchment paper or a greased baking tray. The mixture is soft yet should hold its shape when put on the tray. If it is too soggy, add a teaspoon of potato starch or cornstarch, stir, and wait a few moments for it to firm up. Try scooping them again.

- Bake at 350°F (180°C, or gas mark 4) for 30 to 40 minutes. The outside will develop a golden brown color and become crispy. It is nice to turn the balls over during cooking, but do not attempt to force them off the bottom of the pan before they release themselves or the crust will tear. The insides are very creamy and tender.

GEORGIA

} # RUBY BEET BALLS

Yield: *13 large veggieballs; 4 servings*

14 ounces (390 g) raw beets, peeled
½ of a large red onion
1 can (15 ounces, or 425 g) chickpeas, rinsed (about 1½ cups [390 g])
1 cup (120 g) chopped walnuts
¾ cup (135 g) cooked beet greens or spinach, with the water squeezed out
2 tablespoons (14 g) ground flax seed
⅛ teaspoon red pepper
½ teaspoon dried sage, or 2 teaspoons fresh
1 teaspoon fennel seed
3 tablespoons (45 ml) olive oil
1½ teaspoons salt
¼ teaspoon black pepper
Aged balsamic vinegar, for serving

- Chop the peeled beets and onion into pieces to fit in a food processor (see Tip). Pulse the beets and onion until they are finely chopped, with no large pieces. Dump the beet pulp into a metal or glass mixing bowl. Pulse the chickpeas until they are finely chopped, the same size as the beet mixture. Dump them into the same mixing bowl. Do the same with the walnuts. Add the spinach, flax, red pepper, herbs, olive oil, salt, and pepper.

- Preheat the oven to 350°F (180°C, or gas mark 4). Line a baking tray with parchment paper.

- Mix all the ingredients using a strong spoon. When everything is ruby colored from the beets, use an ice cream scoop or your hands to form large compact balls, 3 inches (7.5 cm) across. Place the balls on the prepared tray and bake for 40 minutes. When done, the outsides will have a firm crust, the bottoms will be brown, and the balls will still appear red.

- Serve with a drizzle of balsamic vinegar and your favorite vegetables.

Beets

Tip:

Instead of a food processor, the beets can be shredded with a box grater or a meat grinder. Use caution and wear an apron; beets stain!

USA

TUSCAN CANNELLINI BEAN BALLS

Yield: *12 medium veggieballs; 4 servings*

FOR THE TOMATO SAUCE:

1 tablespoon (15 ml) olive oil

1 pint cherry tomatoes

2 cloves of garlic, minced

1 can (28 ounces, or 785 g) tomato sauce

Salt and black pepper to taste

FOR THE BEAN BALLS:

1 can (10 ounces, or 280 g) cannellini beans

2 cloves of garlic

1 egg

½ cup (60 g) plain bread crumbs

½ cup (50 g) grated Parmesan cheese

1 teaspoon dried sage (or 1 tablespoon [2 g] fresh)

½ teaspoon salt

½ teaspoon black pepper

Sunflower oil (or canola) for frying

SERVING SUGGESTIONS:

Fresh salad

Cooked pasta or polenta

- To make the sauce, heat the olive oil on high in a pan that can accommodate the sauce. Sauté the cherry tomatoes until blistered and bursting. Stir in the garlic and cook until fragrant. Pour the tomato sauce in, stirring to mix well. Bring to a boil, turn down the heat, and simmer for 5 minutes. Season to taste with salt and fresh ground pepper.

- This makes a thick sauce. If a thinner one is desired, make sauce the same way, adding water until it is the desired consistency.

- To make the bean balls, pulse the beans and garlic in a food processor until they are a chunky paste. Add the egg, bread crumbs, Parmesan cheese, and seasonings; pulse to mix. (If a food processor is unavailable, mince the garlic and use a potato masher to make a paste with the beans.)

- Heat ½ inch (1.3 cm) of oil in a heavy-bottomed pan on medium high. The oil has reached temperature for frying when a small piece of the mixture is dropped in and immediately sizzles and is covered by bubbles. If the oil gets so hot that it smokes, turn the heat down.

- Using a scoop or 2 spoons, form balls of the bean mixture, 2 inches (5 cm) across, about 4 ounces (115 g). Drop them carefully into the oil to avoid splattering. Cook about 1 to 2 minutes before turning, developing a golden brown crust on all sides. Remove from the oil when golden brown and firm. Drain on paper towel.

- Serve the cannellini balls atop the cherry tomato sauce while hot. They are nice with a salad, pasta, or polenta. Try them the next day in sub-style sandwiches.

JAPAN

}

ABUNDANT VEGETABLE TOFU BALLS

in Kombu Broth, "Ganmodoki"

Yield: *10 large veggieballs; 3 servings*

FOR THE TOFU BALLS:

14 ounces (390 g) firm tofu, 1 package
2 to 3 shiitake mushroom caps, finely chopped
1 teaspoon canola oil
1 carrot, shredded
½ cup (55 g) shredded yam or sweet potato
½ sheet of nori seaweed
2 scallions, minced
1 egg white
2 tablespoons (24 g) potato starch or (16 g cornstarch
¾ teaspoon salt

FOR THE KOMBU BROTH:

2 cups (475 ml) water
1 piece kombu, 4 inches (10 cm)
1½ tablespoons (23 ml) soy sauce
1 tablespoon (15 ml) mirin
1 tablespoon (15 ml) sake
A few mushroom stems
1 pinch of sugar

- Drain excess water from the tofu on cloth or paper towels or with a weight on top, such as a cutting board. After draining the tofu for at least 15 minutes, place it in a mixing bowl. With a potato masher or muddler, crush the tofu into small pieces for about 1 minute. The whole thing will look a little bit like cottage cheese.

- In a small pan, cook the mushrooms with the canola oil for 1 to 2 minutes until soft. Add the shredded carrot and yam and cook about 1 minute, just so the rawness is gone and the root vegetables soften a little.

- With scissors, cut the nori sheet into long 1-inch (2.5 cm) strips. Pile these up and cut them the short way, into tiny 1-inch-long (2.5 cm) seaweed confetti.

- Add the nori, scallions, egg white, starch, and salt into the mashed tofu. Stir it all very well until it is all uniform. Line a baking tray with parchment paper and preheat the oven to 350°F (180°C, or gas mark 4). Form golf ball–size balls of the tofu by compressing a portion of it in your hands. Squeeze it into a ball. Don't attempt to "roll" these into balls, they will crumble. Place the balls onto parchment paper, not touching each other.

- Bake for 25 minutes at 350°F (180°C, or gas mark 4). The surface will turn matte and the balls will have bounce. They will still be pale.

- While they bake, make the broth. Place everything in a small pot, simmer for 20 minutes, and strain. Only spoon the broth over the tofu balls immediately before eating because they quickly absorb the liquid and the texture will change.

MIDDLE EAST

} # LENTIL BALLS

with Spices, Lemon Pesto, and Tahini Sauce

Yield: *10 large veggieballs; 3 servings*

FOR THE LENTIL BALLS:

2 cups (475 ml) water

1 cup (192 g) brown lentils

½ cup (70 g) bulgur wheat

1 teaspoon salt

1 teaspoon black pepper

1 teaspoon ground coriander

1 teaspoon ground cinnamon

¼ teaspoon ground cloves

½ teaspoon ground allspice

2 teaspoons ground cumin

1 teaspoon ground cardamom

½ teaspoon ground nutmeg

2 eggs

FOR THE LEMON PESTO:

1 cup fine herbs, such as (60 g) parsley, (16 g cilantro, (40 g) basil, or (96 g) mint

1 teaspoon lemon juice

¼ cup (60 ml) or more olive oil

Pinch of salt

FOR THE TAHINI SAUCE:

¾ cup (180 g) tahini, stirred before measuring

½ cup (120 ml) cold water

Juice from half a lemon

1 clove of garlic, pressed

Pinch of salt

- In a medium saucepan, combine the water and lentils and bring to a boil over high heat. Turn down the heat to the lowest setting, stir, and cover with a lid. Cook for 20 minutes.

- Remove the lid, stir in the bulgur, and replace the lid. Leave to soak for 15 minutes.

- Stir the salt and spices into the lentils and bulgur. When cool enough, mix in the eggs. Squeeze the entire mixture between your fingers for 1 minute.

- Preheat the oven to 350°F (180°C, or gas mark 4). Prepare a baking tray with parchment paper or aluminum foil. Form the lentils into large 3-inch (7.5 cm) balls and place on the baking tray. Bake the lentil balls for 20 to 30 minutes until the outsides are hard and crispy.

- Meanwhile, make the pesto: Place the herbs, lemon juice, oil, and salt in a food processor. Blend until puréed.

- Measure all the tahini sauce ingredients into a glass measuring cup. Stir slowly with a fork. It will appear as if it will never smooth out; keep stirring. At one moment it will emulsify and look velvety. The result should be a thick sauce that pours off a spoon easily. To thin it out, add more water or lemon juice. If it needs thickening, put it in the fridge for 15 minutes or add more tahini. Tahini sauce will keep in the fridge for a week.

- Serve the lentil balls with the pesto and tahini sauce.

JAPAN

} **SCALLION TOFU BALLS**

with Ginger Glaze

Yield: *18 small veggieballs; 4 servings*

FOR THE TOFU BALLS:

1 package (15.5 ounces, or 435 g) extra-firm tofu
1 tablespoon (15 ml) toasted sesame oil
1½ tablespoons (23 ml) soy sauce
1 teaspoon red chili sauce
½ cup (50 g) chopped scallions
1½ tablespoons (24 g) miso paste
½ cup (25 g) panko, Japanese-style bread crumbs

FOR THE GLAZE:

¼ cup (60 ml) sake
¼ cup (60 ml) soy sauce
3 tablespoons (45 g) packed brown sugar
1 tablespoon (15 ml) rice vinegar
½ tablespoon fresh grated ginger

SERVING OPTIONS:

Hot sauce
Cooked rice or noodles

- Dry off the tofu. Place it in a bowl with all the ingredients except the panko. Using a potato masher or a fork, mash the tofu and everything together until the tofu is in small pieces, the size of grains of rice. Resist the urge to overmix it to a paste. Stir in the panko crumbs. Set the mixture aside for 10 minutes.

- Preheat the oven to 375°F (190°C, or gas mark 5). Line a baking tray with parchment paper or oiled aluminum foil.

- Using 2 spoons, form the tofu mash into 1½-inch balls. Line them up on the baking tray, 2 inches (5 cm) apart. Bake for 20 to 25 minutes. The outside will develop a golden brown color, and the tofu balls will have some spring, but will be mostly firm to the touch.

- While they are baking, put the glaze ingredients into a small saucepan. Ginger is best grated on a microplane grater. Boil for 5 minutes. Take off the heat. Serve the tofu balls with the glaze and, if desired, hot sauce. They are nice by themselves or alongside rice or noodles.

UKRAINE

} **POTATO BALLS**

Stuffed with Cheese

Yield: *12 large veggieballs; 4 servings*

½ cup (125 g) ricotta cheese

2 tablespoons (12 g) finely chopped scallions, plus more for serving

1 egg yolk

2¼ cups (506 g) potato, cooked, cooled, mashed

2 tablespoons (24 g) potato starch

3 tablespoons (45 ml) buttermilk

1 egg

¾ teaspoon salt

¾ teaspoon black pepper

Whisper of nutmeg (optional)

- To make the cheese filling, use a fork to mix the ricotta, scallions, egg yolk, and a pinch of salt in a bowl.

- In another bowl, using a fork, mix the cold mashed potato, potato starch, buttermilk, egg, salt, pepper, and nutmeg.

- Bring a pot of salted water to a low simmer on the stove.

- Form a walnut-size ball of potato mixture. While holding it in one palm, make a depression in the ball using a fingertip of the other hand. Place about a teaspoon of cheese filling in the hole. Grab another bit of potato dough to cover up the cheese. Roll it all into a nice neat ball. Repeat until all the potato mixture is formed into balls. (See the description of the stuffing technique on page 10.)

- Poach the balls in batches in the simmering water by lowering them in with a slotted spoon, timing 10 minutes, and removing them to a plate. Ensure the water does not boil, as this can break apart the carefully rolled balls.

- Serve with scallions and fresh ground black pepper.

INDIA

}

ZUCCHINI BALLS

with Tomato Curry Sauce

Yield: *20 medium veggieballs; 4 servings*

FOR THE ZUCCHINI BALLS:

3 big zucchini

1 small onion

½ teaspoon salt

1 teaspoon grated fresh ginger

1 green chile, minced

3 tablespoons (3 g) chopped fresh cilantro

½ cup (60 g) chickpea flour

Vegetable oil for frying

FOR THE CURRY SAUCE:

½ small onion, diced

2 teaspoons vegetable oil

1 tablespoon (15 g) Indian curry paste

½ of a can (6½ ounces, or 200 ml) of coconut milk

1 can (14 ounces, or 390 g) tomato purée (sauce or strained)

- Grate the zucchini and onion on the big holes of a box grater. The grating attachment on a food processor works okay too. Put the grated veggies in a bowl with the salt and set aside for half an hour to drain.

- Meanwhile, make the curry sauce; in a small saucepan, cook the onion with the oil for about 5 minutes until soft. Add the curry paste and sauté it with the onions for 10 seconds until it sizzles. Stir in the coconut milk and cook for 30 seconds before adding the tomato. Simmer on low heat for 10 minutes to infuse the flavors.

- Squeeze out as much liquid from the zucchini and onions as possible. Do this over a bowl, so you can save the liquid, which is added to the sauce for flavor.

- Add the ginger, chile, and cilantro to the wrung-out zucchini. Sprinkle the chickpea flour over it all. Stir to mix very well. Form into tablespoon-size balls.

- Heat 1 to 2 inches (2.5 to 5 cm) of oil in a skillet or wok for frying. When the oil is hot, lower in a few of the zucchini balls. Fry 2 to 3 minutes, turning at least once, so they turn golden brown all over. Remove with a slotted spoon to drain on paper towels.

- Serve the zucchini hot, drizzled or dipped into the curry sauce.

MUSHROOM GARLIC TOFU BALLS

in Tomato Sauce

Yield: *20 medium veggieballs; 4 servings*

FOR THE TOFU BALLS:

14 ounces (390 g) extra-firm tofu, drained
2 tablespoons (28 ml) olive oil
1 small yellow onion, sliced
2 cups (140 g) sliced mushrooms
4 cloves of garlic
¼ teaspoon red pepper flakes
¾ teaspoon salt
¼ cup (30 g) dry bread crumbs
1 tablespoon (4 g) fresh parsley
½ teaspoon ground black pepper
1 egg

FOR COOKING:

Roughly ½ cup (63 g) all-purpose flour
2 tablespoons (28 ml) olive oil
3 cups (735 g) tomato sauce
Parmesan cheese, for serving

- Drain the tofu and press it if necessary. Extra-firm tofu, often sprouted, does not need pressing but can be difficult to find. Firm tofu, which has a higher water content, should be drained in a dish with paper towels and another plate on top for 30 minutes.

- Heat the olive oil in a heavy-bottomed skillet, cook the onions until translucent, and add the mushrooms, garlic, red pepper flakes, and salt. Cook, stirring often, until the mushrooms are tender and glossy, about 5 minutes.

- Transfer the mushroom mixture into the bowl of a food processor. Add the bread crumbs, parsley, pepper, and tofu to the mushroom mixture. Pulse several times to mix. Crack the egg into the mixture and pulse until everything is well incorporated into a rough paste.

- Pour the flour onto a plate. Remove the blade from the food processor for safety. Form the tofu and mushroom mixture into 2-inch (5 cm) balls by first wetting your hands with water so it is less sticky. Gently drop the formed balls into flour, rolling them around to cover all sides. Remove onto waxed paper to avoid sticking. Repeat with all the tofu mixture.

- Heat the olive oil in a heavy-bottomed skillet that can eventually accommodate all the balls in 1 layer. Fry the tofu balls in 2 or 3 batches until golden on many sides, taking care not to crowd the pan so the balls can be rolled over easily. When golden brown, remove the balls gently with a spoon. They are delicate at this stage and firm up when cooked in the sauce. Return all the tofu balls to the pan, cover with the tomato sauce, and simmer on very low heat for 30 minutes. If the sauce becomes too thick while cooking, add a little water. The tofu balls firm up when cooked; test one to check.

- Serve with generous amounts of Parmesan cheese. These make a delicious vegetarian option for a spaghetti and meatball dinner. Don't let the tofu scare you; they don't taste of it at all. Even meat eaters love these.

Resources

Alford, Jeffrey, and Naomi Duguid. *Hot Sour Salty Sweet: A Culinary Journey through Southeast Asia*. New York, NY: Artisan, 2000.

Baljekar, Mridula. *Great Indian Feasts: 130 Wonderful, Simple Recipes for Every Festive Occasion*. London: John Blake Publishers, 2005.

Bayless, Rick. *Mexico: One Plate at a Time*. New York, NY: Scribner, 2000.

Bianchi, Anne. *From the Tables of Tuscan Women: Recipes and Traditions*. Hopewell, NJ: The Ecco Press, 1995.

Bullock, Helen. *The Williamsburg Art of Cookery*. Williamsburg, VA: The Colonial Williamsburg Foundation, 1938 and 1966.

Burton, David. *The Raj at Table: A Culinary History of the British in India*. London: Faber and Faber, 1993.

Child, Julia, Simone, Beck, and Louise Bertholle. *Mastering the Art of French Cooking*. USA: Alfred A. Knopf, Inc., 1961.

Collin, Rima and Richard. *The New Orleans Cookbook*. New York, NY: Alfred A Knopf, Inc., 1975 and 1987.

Cwierczakiewiczowa, Lucyna. *365 Obiadów (365 Dinners)*. Warsaw: Naklad Jana Fiszera, 1911.

De Monteiro, Longteine, and Katherine Neustadt. *The Elephant Walk Cookbook: The Exciting World of Cambodian Cuisine from the Nationally Acclaimed Restaurant*. New York, NY: Houghton Mifflin Co., 1998.

Goldstein, Darra. *The Georgian Feast: The Vibrant Culture and Savory Food of the Republic of Georgia*. New York, NY: HarperCollins Publishers, Inc., 1993.

Harris, Jessica B. *The Africa Cookbook: Tastes of a Continent*. New York, NY: Simon & Schuster, 1998.

Hazan, Marcella. *Essentials of Classic Italian Cooking*. New York, NY: Alfred A. Knopf, Inc., 1992.

King, Niloufer Ichaporia. *My Bombay Kitchen: Traditional and Modern Parsi Home Cooking*. Oakland, CA: University of California Press, 2007.

Kochilas, Diane. *The Glorious Food of Greece: Traditional Recipes from the Islands, Cities, and Villages*. New York, NY: HarperCollins Publishers, Inc., 2001.

Neal, Bill. *Bill Neal's Southern Cooking*. Chapel Hill, NC: The University of North Carolina Press, 1989.

Ortiz, Elizabeth Lambert. *The Food of Spain and Portugal: The Complete Iberian Cuisine*. New York, NY: Atheneum, 1989.

Ottolenghi, Yotam, and Sami Tamimi. *Jerusalem: A Cookbook*. Berkeley, CA: Ten Speed Press, 2012.

Plum, Camilla. *The Scandinavian Kitchen: 100 Essential Ingredients with 200 Authentic Recipes*. Lanham, MD: Kyle Books, Ltd., 2011.

Ramineni, Shubhra. *Entice with Spice: Easy Indian Recipes for Busy People*. Tuttle Publishing, 2010.

Risley, Mary S. *Tante Marie's Cooking School Cookbook: More Than 250 Recipes for the Passionate Home Cook*. New York, NY: Simon & Schuster, 2003.

Salaman, Rena. *Greek Food: An Affectionate Celebration of Traditional Recipes.* London: HarperCollins Publishers, Ltd., 1993.

Samuelsson, Marcus. *The Soul of a New Cuisine: A Discovery of the Foods and Flavors of Africa.* New York, NY: Houghton Mifflin Harcourt Publishing Co., 2006.

Sortun, Ana. *Spice: Favors of the Eastern Mediterranean.* New York, NY: HarperCollins Publishers, Inc., 2006.

Strybel, Robert and Maria. *Polish Heritage Cookery.* New York, NY: Hippocrene Books, Inc., 1993.

Turgeon, Charlotte. *Tante Marie's French Kitchen.* Trans. Rogers, Ann. London: Nicholas Kaye, 1963.

Walker, Ann and Larry. *A Season in Spain.* New York, NY: Simon & Schuster, 1992.

Webster, Cassandra, and The National Council of Negro Women, Inc. *Mother Africa's Table: A Collection of West African and African American Recipes and Cultural Traditions.* New York, NY: Doubleday, 1998.

Index

Abundant Vegetable Tofu Balls in Kombu Broth, 156

Agedashi Tofu. *See* Puffy Fried Tofu Balls, 140

Albondigas with Tomato Sauce, 52

alligator. *See* Louisiana Alligator Meatball Gumbo, 34

Ancient Rome. *See* Jewel-Stuffed Bison Meatballs with Mustard Glaze, 60

Arctic Circle Elk Meatballs, 74

Argentina. *See* Grilled Beef Meatballs with Chimichurri Sauce, 55

Australia
  Beer-Battered Fish Balls with Chili Dipping Sauce, 106
  Grilled BBQ Meatballs, 57
  Orange Duck Meatballs with Celery Root Purée, 94
  Quick Potato, Corn, and Tuna Fish Balls, 131

bacon
  Bacon and Onion Meatball Sliders, 39
  Cassoulet with Duck Confit and Pork Meatballs, 36–37
  Grilled BBQ Meatballs, 57
  Nose to Tail Offal Meatballs, 77
  Venison Meatballs with Wild Berries, 71

Báhn Mi Meatball Sandwich on Baguette, 42

Baked Fish Balls with Frankfurt Green Sauce, 121

Baked Yogurt Sauce, 53

beef
  Albondigas with Tomato Sauce, 52
  Apple and Fennel Kotlecky, 64
  Arctic Circle Elk Meatballs, 74
  Bacon and Onion Meatball Sliders, 39
  Buckwheat Meatballs, 70
  Bulgur and Lamb Meatball Snacks, 18
  Cajun Meatball Stew, 38
  Easy Yellow Curry with Thai Meatballs, 28
  Grilled Apricot and Ostrich Kebabs, 63
  Grilled BBQ Meatballs, 57
  Grilled Beef Meatballs, 55
  Italian Wedding Soup, 24
  Jewel-Stuffed Bison Meatballs with Mustard Glaze, 60
  Little Italy Spaghetti and Meatballs, 51
  Meatball Chowder, 35

Meatball Kebabs, 56

Meatballs with Tomato Sauce, 48

Melting Messy Meatball Sub, 47

Open-Faced Meatball Sandwich, 45

Picnic Favorite Spiced Frikkadels, 22

Poached Meatballs in Caper Cream Sauce, 66

Rich Meatballs and Gravy, 76

Spiced Meatball, Yam, and Peanut Stew over Couscous, 33

Spicy Sichuan Meatballs, 65

Swedish Meatballs, 69

bison. *See* Jewel-Stuffed Bison Meatballs with Mustard Glaze, 60

boar. *See* Poached Meatballs in Caper Cream Sauce, 66

Bolón de Verde. *See* Green Plantain and Cheese Balls, 142

Brazil
  Bulgur and Lamb Meatball Snacks, 18
  Codfish Fritters with Green Brazilian Rice, 126–127
  Xim Xim Nutty Chicken Meatball and Shrimp Stew, 82

Buckwheat Meatballs, 70

Bulgur and Lamb Meatball Snacks, 18

Buñelos de Bacala. *See* Salted Codfish Fritters, 102

Cajun Meatball Stew, 38

Cambodia. *See* Lemongrass Pork Meatball Soup, 30

Caper Cream Sauce, 66

Caribbean. *See* Fish and Yucca Dumplings with Callaloo, 111

Cassoulet with Duck Confit and Pork Meatballs, 36–37

Catfish Hush Puppies with Coleslaw, 120

Celery Root Purée, 94

cheese
  Albondigas with Tomato Sauce, 52
  Bacon and Onion Meatball Sliders, 39
  Chicken Meatballs with Olives, Feta, and Sun-Dried Tomatoes, 87
  Green Plantain and Cheese Balls, 142
  Italian Wedding Soup, 24
  Little Italy Spaghetti and Meatballs, 51

Lobster and Grits Croquettes with Garlic Leafy Greens, 137

Meatballs with Tomato Sauce, 48

Mushroom Garlic Tofu Balls in Tomato Sauce, 166

Next Day Baked Arancini, 148

Potato Balls Stuffed with Cheese, 163

Sicilian Tuna Balls with Roasted Tomatoes, 136

Tuscan Cannellini Bean Balls, 155

Chermoula Sauce
  Chermoula Chicken Boulettes, 90
  Monkfish Balls in a Tagine of Tomato, Olives, and Preserved Lemon, 114
  Moroccan Chard and Chickpeas Fish Ball Tagine, 113

chicken
  Chermoula Chicken Boulettes, 90
  Chicken Meatballs with Olives, Feta, and Sun-Dried Tomatoes, 87
  Deconstructed Red Kubbeh Soup with Couscous, 27
  Japanese Yakitori Chicken Meatballs, 86
  Louisiana Alligator Meatball Gumbo, 34
  Mama's Chicken Meatball Soup, 80
  Red Curry with Eggplant, Greens, and Meatballs, 85
  Red Pozole with Chicken Meatballs, 81
  Taco Chicken Meatballs with Red Salsa Rice, 88
  Xim Xim Nutty Chicken Meatball and Shrimp Stew, 82
  Yellow Gundi Chicken Meatball Soup, 83

Chili Dipping Sauce, 41

Chili Sauce, 106

Chimichurri Sauce, 55

China
  Crunchy Wild Shrimp Balls, 100
  Lion's Head Meatballs, 23
  Spicy Sichuan Meatballs, 65

Chorizo and White Wine Tapas Meatballs, 16

Codfish Fritters with Green Brazilian Rice, 126–127

Costa Rica. *See* Sopa de Albondigas, 31

crab. *See* San Francisco Crab Ball Chowder, 117

Cranberry Sauce, 93

crawfish. *See* Lobster and Grits Croquettes with Garlic Leafy Greens, 137
Crunchy Wild Shrimp Balls, 100
Cuba. *See* Fish Hash Balls, 103
Cucumber Mint Yogurt Dip, 21

Deconstructed Red Kubbeh Soup with Couscous, 27
Denmark. *See* Open-Faced Meatball Sandwich, 45
duck
   Cassoulet with Duck Confit and Pork Meatballs, 36–37
   Duck Curry Meatballs with Spicy Onion Chutney, 97
   Duck, Prosciutto, and Prune Stuffed Meatballs, 91
   Orange Duck Meatballs with Celery Root Purée, 94

Easy Yellow Curry with Thai Meatballs, 28
Ecuador. *See* Green Plantain and Cheese Balls, 142
elk. *See* Arctic Circle Elk Meatballs, 74
emu. *See* Grilled Apricot and Ostrich Kebabs, 63
England
   Lamb and Apricot Meatballs with Greek Yogurt, 75
   Nose to Tail Offal Meatballs, 77

Falafel with Mint Yogurt Sauce, 151
fish. *See also* shellfish.
   Baked Fish Balls with Frankfurt Green Sauce, 121
   Beer-Battered Fish Balls with Chili Dipping Sauce, 106
   Catfish Hush Puppies with Coleslaw, 120
   Codfish Fritters with Green Brazilian Rice, 126–127
   deep frying, 13
   Fish Albondigas in Poblano Salsa, 128
   Fish and Yucca Dumplings with Callaloo, 111
   Fish Ball and Noodle Soup, 118
   Fish Hash Balls, 103
   Fiskeboller, 123

freezing, 11
Fried Fish Balls with Grilled Pineapple Salsa, 105
Ginger and Scallion Namero Mackerel Balls, 132
Herbed Swordfish Balls, 124
Kerala Red Curry with Fish Balls, 109
Monkfish Balls in a Tagine of Tomato, Olives, and Preserved Lemon, 114
Moroccan Chard and Chickpeas Fish Ball Tagine, 113
New England Codfish Balls with Tartar Sauce, 125
Onigiri Rice Balls with Smoked Salmon and Sesame Seeds, 147
Poached Meatballs in Caper Cream Sauce, 66
Poached Salmon Balls, 135
Quick Potato, Corn, and Tuna Fish Balls, 131
Salted Codfish Fritters, 102
Sicilian Tuna Balls with Roasted Tomatoes, 136
Spicy Fish Balls in Tomato Vegetable Stew, 110
Tonga Yam and Fish Fritters with Mango Salsa, 129
France
   Cassoulet with Duck Confit and Pork Meatballs, 36–37
   Provençal Rabbit and Sage Meatballs with Roasted Garlic Aioli and Potatoes, 72–73
   Rich Meatballs and Gravy, 76
Fried Fish Balls with Grilled Pineapple Salsa, 105
Frikadeller Smørrebrød. *See* Open-Faced Meatball Sandwich, 45

Ganmodoki. *See* Abundant Vegetable Tofu Balls in Kombu Broth, 156
Georgia. *See* Ruby Beet Balls, 153
Germany
   Baked Fish Balls with Frankfurt Green Sauce, 121
   Poached Meatballs in Caper Cream Sauce, 66
Ginger and Chile Lentil Fritters, 143

Ginger and Scallion Namero Mackerel Balls, 132
goat
   Easy Yellow Curry with Thai Meatballs, 28
   Meatball Chowder, 35
Greece
   Herbed Swordfish Balls, 124
   Lamb Meatballs with Baked Yogurt Sauce, 53
Green Kofta Curry, 62
Green Plantain and Cheese Balls, 142
Grilled Apricot and Ostrich Kebabs, 63
Grilled BBQ Meatballs, 57
Grilled Beef Meatballs, 55

heart. *See* Nose to Tail Offal Meatballs, 77
Herbed Swordfish Balls, 124

India
   Duck Curry Meatballs with Spicy Onion Chutney, 97
   Ginger and Chile Lentil Fritters, 143
   Green Kofta Curry, 62
   Kerala Red Curry with Fish Balls, 109
   North Indian Potato and Lamb Kofta, 19
   Steamed Spicy Mussel Balls of Mumbai, 108
   Zucchini Balls with Tomato Curry Sauce, 164
Israel. *See* Smoky, Spiced Sumac Meatballs, 61
Italian Wedding Soup, 24
Italy
   Meatballs with Tomato Sauce, 48
   Next Day Baked Arancini, 148
   Sicilian Tuna Balls with Roasted Tomatoes, 136

Japan
   Abundant Vegetable Tofu Balls in Kombu Broth, 156
   Ginger and Scallion Namero Mackerel Balls, 132
   Japanese Yakitori Chicken Meatballs, 86
   Onigiri Rice Balls with Smoked Salmon and Sesame Seeds, 147
   Puffy Fried Tofu Balls, 140
   Scallion Tofu Balls with Ginger Glaze, 160

Jewel-Stuffed Bison Meatballs with Mustard Glaze, 60

Jewish
  Deconstructed Red Kubbeh Soup with Couscous, 27
  Smoky, Spiced Sumac Meatballs, 61
  Vegetarian Matzo Ball Soup, 150

kangaroo. *See* Grilled BBQ Meatballs, 57
Kerala Red Curry with Fish Balls, 109
Ketzitzot. *See* Smoky, Spiced Sumac Meatballs, 61
kidney. *See* Nose to Tail Offal Meatballs, 77
Konigsberg Klopse. *See* Poached Meatballs in Caper Cream Sauce, 66
Korea. *See* Fish Ball and Noodle Soup, 118

lamb
  Bulgur and Lamb Meatball Snacks, 18
  Deconstructed Red Kubbeh Soup with Couscous, 27
  Green Kofta Curry, 62
  Grilled Apricot and Ostrich Kebabs, 63
  Lamb and Apricot Meatballs with Greek Yogurt, 75
  Lamb Meatballs with Baked Yogurt Sauce, 53
  Meatball Kebabs, 56
  North Indian Potato and Lamb Kofta, 19
  Pistachio Lamb Meatballs with Sweet and Sour Pomegranate Glaze, 58
  Pita Sandwiches with Lamb Kefta, Harissa, and Chopped Salad, 44
  Sesame Lamb Meatballs with Cucumber Mint Yogurt Dip, 21
  Smoky, Spiced Sumac Meatballs, 61
Laos. *See* Pork Meatballs in Lettuce Cups with Chili Dipping Sauce, 41
Lemongrass Pork Meatball Soup, 30
Lentil Balls with Spices, Lemon Pesto, and Tahini Sauce, 159
Lion's Head Meatballs, 23
Little Italy Spaghetti and Meatballs, 51
liver. *See* Nose to Tail Offal Meatballs, 77
Lobster and Grits Croquettes with Garlic Leafy Greens, 137
Louisiana Alligator Meatball Gumbo, 34

Mama's Chicken Meatball Soup, 80
Mango Salsa, 129
Meatball Chowder, 35
Meatball Kebabs, 56
Meatballs with Tomato Sauce, 48
Mediterranean. *See* Chicken Meatballs with Olives, Feta, and Sun-Dried Tomatoes, 87
Melting Messy Meatball Sub, 47
Mexico
  Fish Albondigas in Poblano Salsa, 128
  Red Pozole with Chicken Meatballs, 81

Taco Chicken Meatballs with Red Salsa Rice, 88
Middle East
  Falafel with Mint Yogurt Sauce, 151
  Lentil Balls with Spices, Lemon Pesto, and Tahini Sauce, 159
  Pistachio Lamb Meatballs with Sweet and Sour Pomegranate Glaze, 58
  Red Lentil and Bulgur Kufteh in Lettuce Leaves, 146
  Sesame Lamb Meatballs with Cucumber Mint Yogurt Dip, 21
mincemeat. *See* Poached Meatballs in Caper Cream Sauce, 66
Mongolia. *See* Meatball Chowder, 35
Monkfish Balls in a Tagine of Tomato, Olives, and Preserved Lemon, 114
Morocco
  Chermoula Chicken Boulettes, 90
  Moroccan Chard and Chickpeas Fish Ball Tagine, 113
  Pita Sandwiches with Lamb Kefta, Harissa, and Chopped Salad, 44
  Walnut, Za'atar, and Eggplant Kufteh, 144
Mushroom Garlic Tofu Balls in Tomato Sauce, 166
Mushroom Gravy, 70
mussels
  San Francisco Crab Ball Chowder, 117
  Steamed Spicy Mussel Balls of Mumbai, 108
mutton. *See* Meatball Chowder, 35

New England Codfish Balls with Tartar Sauce, 125
Next Day Baked Arancini, 148
North Indian Potato and Lamb Kofta, 19
Nose to Tail Offal Meatballs, 77

offal. *See* Nose to Tail Offal Meatballs, 77
Onigiri Rice Balls with Smoked Salmon and Sesame Seeds, 147
Open-Faced Meatball Sandwich, 45
Orange Duck Meatballs with Celery Root Purée, 94
ostrich. *See* Grilled Apricot and Ostrich Kebabs, 63

Persia. *See* Yellow Gundi Chicken Meatball Soup, 83
Picnic Favorite Spiced Frikkadels, 22
Pistachio Lamb Meatballs, 58
Pita Sandwiches with Lamb Kefta, Harissa, and Chopped Salad, 44
Poached Meatballs in Caper Cream Sauce, 66
Poached Salmon Balls, 135
Poblano Salsa, 128
Poland. *See* Buckwheat Meatballs with Mushroom Gravy, 70

pork
  Apple and Fennel Kotlecky, 64
  Báhn Mi Meatball Sandwich on Baguette, 42
  Buckwheat Meatballs with Mushroom Gravy, 70
  Cajun Meatball Stew, 38
  Cassoulet with Duck Confit and Pork Meatballs, 36–37
  Chorizo and White Wine Tapas Meatballs, 16
  Easy Yellow Curry with Thai Meatballs, 28
  Green Kofta Curry, 62
  Italian Wedding Soup, 24
  Lemongrass Pork Meatball Soup, 30
  Lion's Head Meatballs, 23
  Melting Messy Meatball Sub, 47
  Nose to Tail Offal Meatballs, 77
  Open-Faced Meatball Sandwich, 45
  Picnic Favorite Spiced Frikkadels, 22
  Poached Meatballs in Caper Cream Sauce, 66
  Pork Meatballs in Lettuce Cups with Chili Dipping Sauce, 41
  Provençal Rabbit and Sage Meatballs with Roasted Garlic Aioli and Potatoes, 72–73
  Rich Meatballs and Gravy, 76
  Sopa de Albondigas, 31
  Spicy Sichuan Meatballs, 65
  Swedish Meatballs, 69
Potato Ball and Milk Soup, 149
Potato Balls Stuffed with Cheese, 163
prosciutto. *See* Duck, Prosciutto, and Prune Stuffed Meatballs, 91
Provençal Rabbit and Sage Meatballs with Roasted Garlic Aioli and Potatoes, 72–73
Psarokeftethes. *See* Herbed Swordfish Balls, 124
Puffy Fried Tofu Balls, 140

Quick Potato, Corn, and Tuna Fish Balls, 131
Quinoa Zucchini and Sweet Potato Balls, 152

rabbit
  Louisiana Alligator Meatball Gumbo, 34
  Provençal Rabbit and Sage Meatballs with Roasted Garlic Aioli and Potatoes, 72–73
Red Curry with Eggplant, Greens, and Meatballs, 85
Red Lentil and Bulgur Kufteh in Lettuce Leaves, 146
Red Pozole with Chicken Meatballs, 81
Rich Meatballs and Gravy, 76
Rome. *See* Jewel-Stuffed Bison Meatballs with Mustard Glaze, 60
Ruby Beet Balls, 153

Russia
  Apple and Fennel Kotlecky, 64
  Potato Ball and Milk Soup, 149

Salted Codfish Fritters, 102
San Francisco Crab Ball Chowder, 117
sausage
  Chorizo and White Wine Tapas Meatballs, 16
  Louisiana Alligator Meatball Gumbo, 34
  Rich Meatballs and Gravy, 76
Scallion Tofu Balls with Ginger Glaze, 160
Scandinavia
  Arctic Circle Elk Meatballs, 74
  Fiskeboller, 123
  Poached Salmon Balls, 135
Sesame Lamb Meatballs, 21
shellfish. *See also* fish.
  Crunchy Wild Shrimp Balls, 100
  Lobster and Grits Croquettes with Garlic Leafy Greens, 137
  Louisiana Alligator Meatball Gumbo, 34
  San Francisco Crab Ball Chowder, 117
  Steamed Spicy Mussel Balls of Mumbai, 108
  Xim Xim Nutty Chicken Meatball and Shrimp Stew, 82
shrimp
  Crunchy Wild Shrimp Balls, 100
  Lobster and Grits Croquettes with Garlic Leafy Greens, 137
  Louisiana Alligator Meatball Gumbo, 34
  Xim Xim Nutty Chicken Meatball and Shrimp Stew, 82
Sicilian Tuna Balls with Roasted Tomatoes, 136
Smoky, Spiced Sumac Meatballs, 61
Sopa de Albondigas, 31
South Africa
  Grilled Apricot and Ostrich Kebabs, 63
  Picnic Favorite Spiced Frikkadels, 22
Southern India. *See* Kerala Red Curry with Fish Balls, 109
Southern Italy. *See* Meatballs with Tomato Sauce, 48
South Pacific. *See* Tonga Yam and Fish Fritters with Mango Salsa, 129
Spain
  Chorizo and White Wine Tapas Meatballs, 16
  Salted Codfish Fritters, 102
  Tapas Chickpea Balls, 145
  Spiced Meatball, Yam, and Peanut Stew over Couscous, 33
  Spicy Fish Balls in Tomato Vegetable Stew, 110
Spicy Onion Chutney, 97
Spicy Sichuan Meatballs, 65
Steamed Spicy Mussel Balls of Mumbai, 108

Sweden. *See* Swedish Meatballs, 69
Sweet and Sour Pomegranate Glaze, 58

Taco Chicken Meatballs with Red Salsa Rice, 88
Tahini Sauce, 159
Tapas Chickpea Balls, 145
Tartar Sauce, 125
Thailand
  Easy Yellow Curry with Thai Meatballs, 28
  Red Curry with Eggplant, Greens, and Meatballs, 85
Thanksgiving Stuffing Turkey Meatballs with Cranberry Sauce, 93
tips and tricks
  cooking, 10
  deep-frying, 13
  formation, 10
  freezing, 11
  grinding, 13
  stuffing, 10
Tonga Yam and Fish Fritters with Mango Salsa, 129
Tunisia. *See* Monkfish Balls in a Tagine of Tomato, Olives, and Preserved Lemon, 114
Turkey. *See* Meatball Kebabs, 56
Tuscan Cannellini Bean Balls, 155

Ukraine
  Mama's Chicken Meatball Soup, 80
  Potato Balls Stuffed with Cheese, 163
USA
  Bacon and Onion Meatball Sliders, 39
  Cajun Meatball Stew, 38
  Catfish Hush Puppies with Coleslaw, 120
  Duck, Prosciutto, and Prune Stuffed Meatballs, 91
  Fried Fish Balls with Grilled Pineapple Salsa, 105
  Italian Wedding Soup, 24
  Little Italy Spaghetti and Meatballs, 51
  Lobster and Grits Croquettes with Garlic Leafy Greens, 137
  Louisiana Alligator Meatball Gumbo, 34
  Melting Messy Meatball Sub, 47
  Mushroom Garlic Tofu Balls in Tomato Sauce, 166
  New England Codfish Balls with Tartar Sauce, 125
  Quinoa Zucchini and Sweet Potato Balls, 152
  San Francisco Crab Ball Chowder, 117
  Thanksgiving Stuffing Turkey Meatballs with Cranberry Sauce, 93
  Tuscan Cannellini Bean Balls, 155
  Venison Meatballs with Wild Berries, 71

veal
  Nose to Tail Offal Meatballs, 77
  Open-Faced Meatball Sandwich, 45

Poached Meatballs in Caper Cream Sauce, 66
  Smoky, Spiced Sumac Meatballs, 61
  Swedish Meatballs, 69
Vegetarian Matzo Ball Soup, 150
Venezuela. *See* Albondigas with Tomato Sauce, 52
venison
  Arctic Circle Elk Meatballs, 74
  Venison Meatballs with Wild Berries, 71
Vietnam. *See* Báhn Mi Meatball Sandwich on Baguette, 42

Walnut, Za'atar, and Eggplant Kufteh, 144
West Africa
  Spiced Meatball, Yam, and Peanut Stew over Couscous, 33
  Spicy Fish Balls in Tomato Vegetable Stew, 110

Xim Xim Nutty Chicken Meatball and Shrimp Stew, 82

Yellow Gundi Chicken Meatball Soup, 83

Zucchini Balls with Tomato Curry Sauce, 164

Acknowledgments

This collection of meatballs wouldn't have happened if it wasn't for my editor, Jonathan. Michael, my chief meatball tester and support, thank you for being there through this project! Thank you to all my recipe and meatball testers, Miranda, Sue and Trip, Jennie, Scott, Chloe, Tim, Julie, Halyna, Henry, Lauren, Nancy, Ann, and John. Special thanks to Marianna for translating her grandparents' Polish meatball recipe. And to the Schullers, who shared their meatball recipes and stories to go with them. And I need to extend thanks to Marcus Samuelsson and Yotam Ottolenghi who emboldened me to utilize my spice shelf in brave new ways, without which I would not have had the courage to undertake this meatball journey.

I was fortunate to spend time with the wonderful collection of historical cookbooks and sunny reading rooms at the Boston Athenaeum. And I am grateful for all the people who openly share memories of food and recipes in the marginalia of comment sections on the Web. I found many great leads on what some of the old-fashioned recipes found here should taste like. Recipes change as families move to new countries and languages and methods of food production shift. Getting to the heart of a flavor or ingredient was often helped by somebody's memory of their grandmother's soup or their uncle's spice blend. I hope that this sharing continues, for it makes us all richer in our connected history of food.

About the Author

Adeline Myers teaches cooking and writes about food in Salem, Massachusetts. Passionate about sustainability and healthy eating, she seeks out the freshest local foods. Culinary book clubs, travel, and a growing collection of antique cookbooks keep her inspired in the kitchen. She is a graduate of Smith College and Tante Marie's Cooking School in San Francisco. This is her first cookbook.

Also Available

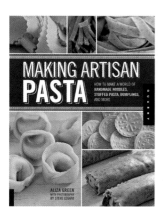

Making Artisan Pasta
978-1-59253-732-7

Making Soda at Home
978-1-59253-913-0

Kitchen Workshop—Pizza
978-1-59253-883-6

Noodle Kids
978-1-59253-963-5